Having recently obtained my master's in psychology, I was faced with the decision of becoming a licensed therapist or certified as a coach. *From Therapist to Coach* was an excellent and timely resource that inspired and helped me make my decision, and I am currently in the process of becoming a certified coach. Thanks, David!

—Colette Kenney, MA, Calgary, Alberta, Canada

From Therapist to Coach is well written, clear, concise, and thought provoking. I highly recommend it to any clinician interested in coaching. It is full of great information for the aspiring coach and full of tips that will save time and money in pursuing a coaching practice. The marketing chapters in particular are brilliant and confidence building.

—Valee More, The Oasis Clinic, Auckland, New Zealand

This book is very practical and helpful to the therapist who wants to make a change and feels a bit overwhelmed with the possibilities. The section on choosing a niche was illuminating and very exciting to me. I found it helpful to have the training options outlined so clearly, and the marketing section was extremely useful as well. Thank you for pioneering this transition for those of us who feel it is time to make a change.

—Shelley R. Cohen, LCSW, Beverly Hills, CA

From Therapist to Coach is bursting with invaluable, practical considerations and recommendations. I highly recommended this book as the definitive resource for therapists who are curious about coaching. David Steele has crafted a marvelous insider guide to the tricky and delicate art of introducing and integrating coaching to your practice. Its concise nature appealed to me, while simultaneously it is so thoroughly comprehensive in its exploration of all considerations.

This book has sparked a renewed passion for my work as I have struggled the past couple of years with how to incorporate coaching into my psychotherapy practice. I knew there must be a way to do it but lacked the "how to." Based on his years of experience and real insight, David Steele supplies the necessary tools to do so effectively as well as invaluable strategies to help avoid the pitfalls. I can finally move forward now in developing a profitable, solid practice as a coach without compromising or conflicting who I am as a therapist. I've already made some excellent progress as a result of reading this book. Without hesitation, I highly recommend this as a book that you will return to time and time again as a handbook for your private practice as a therapist/coach.

—Sharon O'Farrell, MIHA, Navan, Ireland

Clinicians can make some of the best life coaches. The transition from therapist to coach is fraught with challenges to their perceived role as expert and the business of adding a new and distinct professional service to their practice. A real paradigm shift is required that includes both personal and professional development. *From Therapist to Coach* is an invaluable guidebook to aid in this transition. David Steele has made this book practical and readable, and includes excellent advice and tips to create a successful transition to coaching.

—Patrick Williams, EdD, Master Certified Coach, founder of
Institute for Life Coach Training

From Therapist to Coach is the best book about coaching and building a successful coaching practice I've read so far. It's practical, with a solid theoretical foundation and a wealth of knowledge and experience. It is such a pleasure to read for a savvy reader. This book makes a great deal of sense and helps put coaching into perspective by identifying and addressing the potential questions and concerns that might arise for therapists from a traditional therapeutic background and by using useful analogies and practical examples. I absolutely loved this book! It's written with ease, grace, humor, and style, as well as with a great deal of respect and understanding of both worlds.

—Irina Hart, MFT, Melbourne, Australia

FROM
THERAPIST
TO COACH

FROM THERAPIST TO COACH

How to Leverage Your Clinical Expertise to Build a Thriving Coaching Practice

DAVID STEELE

WILEY

John Wiley & Sons, Inc.

Library of Congress Cataloging-in-Publication Data:

Steele, David J. (David Jay), 1948-
    From therapist to coach : how to leverage your clinical expertise to build a thriving
coaching practice / David Steele.
        p.   cm.
    Includes index.
    ISBN 978-0-470-63023-5 (pbk.); ISBN 978-1-118-02540-6 (ebk);
    ISBN 978-1-118-02539-0 (ebk); ISBN 978-1-118-02538-3 (ebk)
        1. Personal coaching.   I. Title.
    BF637.P36S74   2011
    158.1—dc22

                                                                    2010048921

Printed in the United States of America

10 9 8 7 6 5 4 3 2 1

Contents

Preface   *xi*

Acknowledgments   *xix*

CHAPTER ONE

From Frustrated Therapist to Successful Coach   1

A burned-out therapist discovers coaching and builds a successful
coaching business in three months.

CHAPTER TWO

Comparing Coaching and Therapy   11

What is coaching and how is it similar to and different from therapy?
How are therapy clients and a therapy practice different from coaching
clients and a coaching practice?

CHAPTER THREE

How to Become a Coach   37

Do you need coaching training? How do you find training that
doesn't duplicate what you already know? How can you be a coach
and a therapist?

CONTENTS

CHAPTER FOUR

Integrating Coaching into Your Therapy Practice   61

How will you set your fees? Do you need different liability insurance? What are the legal implications? Can you bill medical insurance for coaching? Do you need different forms for coaching? How are coaching sessions different from therapy sessions? Do you market your coaching services differently?

CHAPTER FIVE

Choosing Your Coaching Niche   77

What is a niche? The benefits of choosing a niche. How do you choose a niche? How to own your niche. Can you coach more than one niche?

CHAPTER SIX

Designing Your Service Delivery System   97

How to use market research to guarantee your success. Designing a service delivery system to meet the needs of your niche. How to create packages, programs, and products for your niche.

CHAPTER SEVEN

Marketing Your Coaching Practice   115

What not to do. Does marketing create clients? Marketing versus enrollment. Basic marketing strategies. How to market creatively, effectively, and affordably.

CHAPTER EIGHT

How to Enroll Clients for Your Coaching Practice   151

How getting coaching clients differs from getting therapy clients. Selling versus enrollment. Conducting an effective enrollment conversation. How to get a client whenever you want.

CHAPTER NINE

Building a Successful Coaching Business   165

Becoming an entrepreneur. How to get paid what you're worth. Promoting client loyalty and longevity. Maximizing your private practice income. How to have fun, play large, and retire smiling.

Contents

APPENDICES

A. Selected resources for building your coaching business   175

B. 14 Compelling reasons to use a professional coach   177

C. A short history of coaching for clinicians   181

D. Six stages of client readiness for change   187

E. Beyond psychotherapy: working outside   193
the medical model

ABOUT DAVID STEELE   201

Preface

It doesn't matter where you've been. What matters is where you're going, and how you'll get there.

In the title of this book, the words *therapist* and *coach* are so close together—separated only by the harmless little word *to*—that it's easy to think that the journey from therapist to coach is easy and automatic. Well, it is and it isn't.

Yes, the transition from therapist to coach *is* refreshingly easy when you break it all down into practical steps; but it's hardly automatic. In fact, I'd say that for most therapists, including the one holding this book, the idea of adding coaching to your world probably causes feelings of confusion, skepticism, doubt, and fear.

What's going on? It's like this: Coaching just isn't what most of us had on our career radar screen when we were traveling the long and winding road to licensure. Although I assume you're at least *partially* open to the idea of coaching because you're reading this book, I won't assume that we're out of those skeptical woods just yet.

In other words, though the idea of coaching sparks your curiosity, it may still linger as something inappropriate at worst, impractical at best, and incomprehensible at all times. That's the bad news.

But the *good* news is these feelings are natural and common, because I've felt them, too. Time for a story.

THERE WAS THIS MEN'S GROUP . . .

Early on a cold Saturday morning in 1996, I was standing in a large circle of attendees for the monthly gathering of our men's organization. At one point a youngish man in his 20s, known to me as a health supplement salesman, stepped out and proclaimed something that was so absurd and unexpected that I'm positive I'm going to remember exactly how it sounded for a full year after I die. Here's what this consequence of good ol' American Dreamism had to say: "I'm training to become a life coach, and I'm looking for a few volunteer practice clients!"

Until that moment, although I had read and heard the term *jaw-dropping* more times than I could remember, I had not personally experienced it. (Yes, for the curious playing along at home, your jaw really does drop!) And then other body parts got into action, including my brain, which went into overdrive. Here's the family-friendly version of my inner dialogue: "Life coach—what's that? How can this guy help *anyone* with their life if he can't figure it out for himself? Wait a minute—he's going to charge people money to help them with their lives? But that's what *I* do and I have a degree and a license! Has this guy been sampling one too many health supplements or something?"

But despite the bells going off inside me (I half expected someone to come over and slap me on the head like an alarm clock), I must admit that I was intrigued. Well, okay—*intrigued* is probably a bit too glorious a word, and makes me sound more open-minded than I was. Let's say I was compelled to see this train wreck close up.

So I wandered over to the health supplement salesman/life coach, and asked him what this whole thing was all about. His answer was to try a session with him and find out. I agreed.

The following week, we met on the telephone (the telephone, of all things! Does this train wreck have an *end*?), and he asked me some open-ended questions about what I wanted for my life. He paused long enough after each response to make me think that he had a list of questions in front of him, and was awkwardly searching for the next question to ask. It was like helping one of my kids with their homework by practicing a school assignment with them — except my kids weren't studying to be life coaches. Heck, I almost wished he'd just try to sell me some health supplements. (*Almost.*)

Still, with tolerance that I didn't know I had, I went along with it and talked about my desire to help people have successful marriages and families; my burnout working with dysfunctional couples and feeling stuck with my current practice; and my frustrations, hopes, and dreams for my practice. And as I spoke, something . . . *weird* was happening.

By the end of our unskilled and awkward first meeting, I had gone from feeling burned out and stuck with my practice to feeling excited, empowered, and reenergized. As a therapist I was obliged to categorize this as that thing that we crave, that seminal event that makes everything else possible and all the hard work worth it: a breakthrough. No, wait. That's not fair. It wasn't just a breakthrough. It was A BREAKTHROUGH!!!

That was the moment. That was the handoff. I was *sold* on coaching. If a young, unskilled, brand-new coach trainee could help me (of all people) achieve a breakthrough, think of the possibilities! And imagine my amazement that a brand-new helping profession was emerging right under my nose, and I didn't know anything about it until that fateful Saturday morning with my men's group. Fate sold health supplements in its spare time. Who knew?

I immediately signed up to be trained as a coach, and quickly saw the potential for applying this powerful helping methodology to relationships. My professional career changed forever — and for the better.

IS THIS BOOK FOR YOU?

Okay. You might be thinking: "Hey, that was a really feel-good story, David, but how is your book going to help me? You aren't going to try to sell me some health supplements, are you? Because . . . there's someone at the door . . . I have to take my kid to a thing . . . I'll get back to you next week. . . ." Don't worry. There are no health supplements to buy (honest), and there's a reason you should read this book. Scratch that: There's a reason you *must* read this book. It's this:

A long time ago (possibly in a galaxy far, far away or on a dark and stormy night), you decided to become a therapist. At least that's how it looked to others. But for you, truly, it was a powerful calling in which you didn't have much choice. I still remember my mother saying, "A therapist? You'll never make a living!"

The point is, you decided to dedicate your life to helping people overcome major life problems, achieve important goals, reach their optimal potential, and get to the next level in their lives. So yes, for convenience—and because all this doesn't fit on a business card— you call yourself a therapist. But we both know that the truth is deeper. We know that you wanted to facilitate meaningful, lasting growth and change, and make a significant difference in the world. You wanted to help.

Now here you are, years later, and guess what? You still want to help! And even if you're approaching burnout, your original idealistic flame still burns deep within your serving spirit; you wouldn't be reading a book like this if there wasn't something inside you urging you forward. True, perhaps you can't see that flame as clearly as you once did, but surely if you pay close attention, you can still feel its heat and hear its message. Despite your dissatisfaction with how things are, it's telling you:

- **Yes!** You deserve to experience the personal and professional satisfaction you were promised by your profession.
- **Yes!** Whether you're a specialist or a generalist, there must be a way to recapture the variety, freedom, and flexibility in your work that have been so utterly devoured by the medical/ insurance billing model ("diagnose, treat, bill," and repeat ad nauseum . . . or ad burnout).
- **Yes!** There are motivated, functional people out there who want your help, instead of those who really need the services of a psychiatrist for their clinical disorders.

- **Yes!** There is a way to bridge the disconnect between what you truly want to be (someone who helps create positive change) and how you're perceived (someone who fixes problems).
- **Yes!** You would love to be the provider of first resort when they need support, instead of last resort when they're desperate and it's often too late.
- **Yes!** You want to help people who see the value of your services and are happy to pay for them, instead of those who are willing to work with you only if their insurance pays for it.
- **Yes!** You want to build a solid and profitable business aligned with who you are and why you became a therapist.

If you're nodding at one, some, or probably all of these—and don't feel alone, because this boat is large and filled with more therapists that you may imagine—then **Yes!**, this book is for you. (By the way, I have some health supplements that will help with that nodding . . . just kidding!)

WHAT YOU CAN EXPECT

In a fit of good judgment and common sense that doesn't seem to influence many other books on the market today, this book is written for therapists *by* a therapist. I understand emotionally, intuitively, and intellectually the challenges that you're facing—because I've been there and know what you're going through. Furthermore, this book is written specifically for clinicians in private practice who want to help *people*. It's not written for working with businesses, though the information it presents is meant to be applied to your practice in a business sense.

In a nutshell, here's what you can expect from the pages that follow:

- A clear, organized, friendly, and engaging style that is easy to read and understand for the non-business-minded reader
- Examples and insights that therapists like you can easily (and sometimes humorously) relate to

- A practical approach on how to build a successful business as a coach utilizing traditional and creative strategies, including marketing, getting clients, choosing a niche, and more
- A focus on creative group services and business models suited to the various specialties and niches of personal coaching
- A look at the creative and more profitable models for marketing and service delivery of coaching
- A discussion of the issues, opportunities, and strategies for how you can build a successful business as a coach or therapist/coach
- Coverage of the regulatory obligations facing you as a U.S.–based therapist/coach

Above all, I'd like you to know that this is a practical book, not a theoretical one. True, while we cover issues that are emotional (such as your motivation to become a coach) or abstract (such as the noble role of a helping professional versus what most of us end up *doing* as therapists), the essence of this book is the information and strategies needed to support your transition from therapist to therapist/coach. As such, you can consider this a workbook, guide, or manual for your successful professional future.

What's Inside

In the first few chapters (Chapters 1, 2, and 3), I go straight to the (broken) heart of the matter for most therapists reading this book: Working as a therapist in today's world is just not fulfilling personally or professionally. And if that weren't enough, it's not rewarding financially, either, especially when the bulk of clients are billed through insurance. You'll read how a burned-out therapist (that would be me) was able to build a successful coaching business in three months. I also cover how coaching and its clients are—and are not—similar to therapy and its clients, whether you need training as a coach, how to find the training you might need without duplicating what you already know, and perhaps the biggest question facing some: how to be a coach *and* a therapist at the same time.

Next, in Chapters 4 and 5, I show you how to integrate coaching into your therapy practice. I cover how you can identify if a client needs coaching versus therapy, whether it's beneficial to provide coaching and therapy to the same client, how to set appropriate fees for coaching, whether you need different liability insurance for your coaching, whether you can bill medical insurance for your coaching, and whether you need different forms. I also help you identify your specialty and niche. And if you're not quite sure what these terms are, or how they apply to you, don't worry—I cover that, too.

In the last group of chapters (Chapters 6, 7, 8, and 9), I help you design your service delivery system through market research, programming (the marketing kind, not the computer kind), product integration, and joint ventures, and describe how to leverage technology, time, and income to help your practice get ahead. I also show you how to use creative marketing strategies to define and build your brand, and how to use the Internet and other channels to connect with prospective clients and maintain relationships with your existing ones. I provide you with cost-effective ways to get clients and build a successful coaching business.

A Little Note Before You Begin

Despite your interest and, I would hope, budding or blossoming enthusiasm for becoming a coach, you may still feel hesitant about learning more about coaching. Don't feel alarmed by this. Even for seasoned therapists who advocate for change on a daily basis, the idea of leaving the familiar and embracing the new can be scary, because you may think the journey from therapist to coach is going to be long, and you simply don't feel that there's a finish line here that you can see. Here's something for you to think about:

If I go back in time and put myself right where you are now, I can make this humbling observation: You are much better off than I was! Unlike you, I didn't have a book like this to help me focus my strategies and efforts, and now that coaching has been around for a while, you probably know more about coaching than I did before my first training.

You could say that this is the book I wish *I* had read when I was where you are right now. It'll save you time, money, and hassle, while giving you proven tips and practical steps to move forward. It'll help you avoid some or all of my mistakes, and set you that much further ahead on your way to professional satisfaction. As I'm fond of saying in my workshops and lectures (partly to ruffle the feathers of insight-oriented therapists), "It doesn't matter where you've been. What matters is where you're going, and how you'll get there." This also happens to be my abbreviated definition of coaching.

This is the book that will help you get there. It's designed to reenergize your inner flame, not just because it's what you need, but because it's what the world needs *through* you — now, it seems, more than ever.

Acknowledgments

This book is the culmination of many years of experience and learning that put me in a unique and fortunate position to be able to share this important information with you, my colleagues. I wish to gratefully acknowledge these wonderful people for supporting this book and making it possible:

Relationship Coaching Institute members and staff for their support, input, and being the testing ground for bringing coaching to the mainstream. They are intimately familiar with the evolution of every idea and strategy in this book.

Jason Kalra of Abundant Words, a talented writer whose skills transformed my dry, factual, linear nonfiction text into engaging, fun, easy-to-read prose that caused me to laugh out loud at times (not an easy feat!).

Marquita Flemming, Senior Editor at John Wiley & Sons, who truly gets the importance of coaching. She found her way into the audience of a conference seminar I delivered for therapists about coaching, decided I was the right person to write this book, and supported my efforts every step of the way with wise advice, expert suggestions, and enthusiastic cheerleading.

Darlene Steele, my wife, soul mate, muse, business partner, and sounding board, who witnessed and supported every high and low in the long process of bringing this book from concept to reality.

CHAPTER ONE

From Frustrated Therapist to Successful Coach

A burned-out therapist discovers coaching and builds a successful coaching business in three months.

My journey from therapist to coach was not, I must admit, so much a journey as it was an experiment—except that instead of being in a nice clean lab, wearing a starchy white coat and generally feeling all *experimental*, I was earnestly driving to the only coach training around, and hoping that I'd find something to nourish my budding coaching spirit. Part of me felt that I was flying without a map, part of me wondered if I was setting myself up for severe disappointment, and whatever parts I had left were wondering just what the heck I thought I was doing, anyway.

Fortunately—mercifully, I might say—the training was impressive. And by that I don't mean that it was striking, remarkable, or anything else that my thesaurus tells me is a synonym for the word *impressive*. I mean that it *made an impression* on me—it reshaped my mind, and altered the paradigm that I now, as a successful coach, use regularly.

Here's why: The coaching exercises were nothing short of transforming. For example, one of the earliest exercises was to work with a partner for five minutes, doing nothing but asking questions. That's it: no suggestions, no feedback, no reflective listening, no brilliant insights, no small talk . . . just questions. Sound easy? I thought so, too, until about the, oh, 12-second mark. That's when it hit me: As a therapist, I was trained to listen, assess, and use my clinical judgment to provide feedback and interventions. Yet here as a coach (or a coach in training), I had to ask *powerful* questions that helped the respondent get in touch with his or her own personalized truth, wisdom, and direction. My role as a coach was not to diagnose and treat, but to empower and enable; not to analyze and reduce, but to synthesize and cocreate; not to uncover, but to *discover*. This. Was. Exciting!

It was as if doors and windows in a closed room were blown wide open and fresh air and sunlight were pouring in. Strangely, however, it wasn't as if this was an entirely new experience. There was something familiar about this—and, since my intuition at this time was chugging along like a popcorn machine on uppers, it quickly hit me what this familiarity was: This was the connection—the *alignment*—that had motivated me to become a therapist in the first place. It was blissful.

FROM BLISS TO EPIPHANY

A Zen master is credited with saying, "First ecstasy, then the laundry." And while I'm certainly not a Zen master, I can still paraphrase and say that my next task was to take my *bliss* and apply it in a practical way to my professional life as a couples therapist and (budding) coach.

The first thing I noticed was that this wasn't going to be convenient. That is, there wasn't any template or step-by-step model to follow, nor were there even the building blocks of one. Relationship coaching, as I've come to define it today, *simply didn't exist back in the late 1990s*. Sure, there were folks claiming to be relationship gurus, relationship wizards, relationship experts, and even a few relationship coaches, but there was no standardization for applying this exciting new methodology called "coaching" to relationships. Furthermore, except for coaches trained by programs accredited by the International Coach Federation (ICF), there wasn't even an appreciation for standards. Many people were just doing their own thing and calling it coaching. It was truly a licensing board's worst nightmare.

I had a problem with that. Because, even though I wasn't thrilled with life as a therapist, that didn't mean that I wanted to get rid of my principles, or my belief in the value of professional standards and a way to measure, achieve, and monitor those standards. So I had work to do.

Through the lens of coaching, which I'll discuss more in a moment, I started to view my work in a different light: in a way that was in harmony with the very essence of the helping profession. I started asking myself surprisingly fundamental questions about what I was doing, who I was doing it for, and how I could achieve it. (See, I told you they were fundamental questions.) And during this process, I experienced the biggest epiphany of my life so far. Three little words exploded into my head like flames after a lightning strike: *"Singles become couples."* That's it! This was my *key* to reaching the public, lowering the divorce rate, and getting motivated clients. As a therapist I'd worked with many individuals, but it had never occurred to me to work with singles as a way to promote successful relationships. As a coach, this seemed natural. Because, after all, where do couples come from? They come from singles. It was so simple.

So, even though (at the time) I had no idea how to help them, I started to focus on singles. That is, I relied on straightforward marketing strategies (more on this in a moment) to reach out to singles and, through the lens of coaching, I created systems that enabled singles to find and have healthy, nourishing, and loving relationships. And to my delight, it worked! People from all walks of life—not unhealthy people in search of a cure, but everyday people in search of something *better*—were attending my events, lectures, and workshops. Things became so busy that I started training associates, who could then reach out to more people. In three months, though I still had a few therapy clients, 99% of my time was spent on coaching, and on coaching new coaches (say *that* three times fast).

With the luxury of hindsight, I can say that there were four key ingredients that enabled my success. It's hard to say which was most important and which least; it's easier (and more honest) to say that they all worked interdependently to move me forward. They were:

1. My willingness to put aside my fears and anxieties as a therapist and fully explore something new. It's probable that it would have been easier for me if I *hadn't* been a therapist, because it's sometimes easier to launch into something new when you aren't comparing it to something old.
2. The empowering principles of coaching itself, which I'll focus on later in this chapter.
3. The people around me: the singles who showed up at my events and workshops, and the other coaches and associates who contributed to the vision that became the Relationship Coaching Institute (RCI).
4. My marketing strategies (and guesses and hopes and "let's try this—it can't hurt" tactics). Let's look at these now.

My Marketing Experience . . .
I Mean *Experiment*

Later in this book, I devote a solid chunk of space to easy, practical, and low-cost—sometimes *no-cost*—marketing ideas, all of which I've used with success. For now, however, I'd like to take a smaller look (call it an appetizer, if you wish) at the specific marketing that I experimented with early in my coaching career. As you read these strategies, I'd like you to keep two good things in mind:

1. Yes, marketing *can* be this easy, and you don't already need to be a marketing guru to figure it out.

2. Even if you aren't planning to be a relationship coach (and I don't presume that you are), you can still abstract the strategies I used here and easily apply them to any kind of coaching that you'll do—sports, business, weight loss, helping artists. There's no limit.

Now back to my marketing experiment—and I call it that instead of *experience* because, back then, it was honestly more of an experiment. I needed to find a way to reach out to singles. But how? I wasn't used to this way of doing things. As a therapist, I had relied on my yellow pages ad, managed-care referrals, and word of mouth to build my practice. But as a coach, I had the freedom—and the responsibility— to venture out of my office and be more proactive. For that, I needed marketing. Because that's what marketing is *good* at doing.

Keeping things simple out of necessity more than preference, it occurred to me that finding prospective single clients for my new coaching practice in traditional settings would probably be a mistake. By traditional, I mean singles bars and other places that are, typically, thinly veiled meat markets that attract two types of clientele: predators and the dangerously uninformed. While I empathize with the latter and admit they need help (i.e., they need to *leave* the premises as soon as possible), I needed to look elsewhere. Aha! My men's organization and an affiliated women's organization would be the places to start. That's where my target market could be found; that's where, presumably, I'd connect with singles looking for the tools and support for creating and maintaining successful relationships.

Using old-fashioned tools like my own voice and the telephone, as well as this relatively new thing (at the time) called e-mail, I spread the word about my four-session pilot program for singles: meet in my office as a group every Thursday evening for a month. And just like the Field of Dreams, I built it, and they came. Well, okay, there wasn't a flood of demand. But there wasn't a sad trickle, either. I could fit only 12 people in my office, and all 12 slots were filled within a week after first announcing the program. Though I wasn't fully conscious about my strategy at the time, this became my focus group that helped me understand the goals, needs, and challenges of singles in my area. The attendees' feedback helped me craft a weekly Friday Night Social that was designed to be an alternative to the singles scene, and provided what I billed as a "safe, fun, educational place for singles to meet." It was a positive community resource for singles that helped me connect with prospective coaching clients—everybody benefited.

I scheduled my first Friday Night Social for the following month, marketing it mostly through word of mouth, a few press releases, and some free listings in local newspaper calendar sections. I rented a private, comfortable space in a nearby group practice that could hold up to 25 people, and recruited one of my office mates to help out (thanks, Kathleen!). Nobody worked in the building on Friday nights, so we had the place to ourselves. The first week I was a nervous wreck, fearing that no one would come, and was grateful and excited to have 18 participants. The second week 24 showed up. The third week was standing room only as participants overflowed into the hallways, and I had to scramble to find a larger space for future meetings. My coaching practice was full within three months, and I brought a partner (Marvin Cohen) and some associates on board to manage the growth of our singles community and the demand for our classes, workshops, groups, and individual coaching.

The Friday Night Social was a success and attracted local singles hailing from different walks of life, all looking for empowerment and information. It was inspiring and fun. Word quickly spread, and even fellow therapists were referring their single clients to me and asking me to conduct a training for them. That first training marked the birth of the Relationship Coaching Institute (RCI). Again, I'll take a deeper and less autobiographical look at marketing later in this book. The preceding account was simply to provide you with an idea of how easy it is to pull together.

Now, I'd like to switch gears and refocus on coaching itself. During my training, I discovered (i.e., bumped into, was hit over the head with, was shocked by, and so on) coaching principles that supplied my "aha" moments. They created my new paradigm of doing work and have influenced everything that I've done with RCI. Since these are principles, and not specific to me or my coaching niche, they can work for you, too. So that means that if you're one of those readers who likes to underline things in books, the next part is where you want to have your pencil sharp and at the ready.

FIVE PRINCIPLES OF COACHING

The first principle I discovered is that coaching forces you (and yes, it is a forcing) to note **how people make choices**. This awareness provides you with the basic understanding that the problem *and* the solution are not out there in a diagnosis or a pill, but inside the coached individual himself or herself. The simple key—and it's not an easy key sometimes, but it's clearly a key nonetheless—is to make choices in alignment with desired outcomes. That is, to help individuals see that they are the architects of the very problems they want to solve, and that in each case the problem as well as the solution lies in their choices. Yes, this is difficult for many individuals who want us to fix their problems, but at precisely the same time, it's also very empowering and liberating.

The second principle I discovered is that coaching creates a **developmental question for an individual to answer**. Often, this question is not conveniently literal. In other words, it's not as if an individual can easily articulate the question, "How can I be a more positive creator of my relationships?" Rather, conceptually, the idea of coaching is about reaching into individuals (or more accurately, creating the space and safety for individuals to reach into *themselves*) and discovering what they want to achieve, and what they want to improve upon and develop. Again, this is markedly different from some forms of therapy where the clinical treatment is determined by the diagnosis, which in turn is determined by the therapist consulting the American Psychiatric Association's *Diagnostic and Statistical Manual of Mental Disorders* (*DSM*). In coaching, both the responsibility and the power ultimately lie with the person being coached, not with the therapist. Most therapists agree with this principle and even believe they practice it.

The third principle that I discovered is that coaching **is proactive and about creating positive solutions, not about avoiding**

negative states. This may seem blatantly obvious, but again, remember that these principles are more than just knowledge; put into practice, they will shape how you *apply* coaching in your professional world, just as they did to mine. Overall, this principle posits that individuals are designed to be successful, and that an unsuccessful individual is merely stuck on the road to success. The goal is then to identify the blocks, effectively remove them, and then let the default, natural success resume. Success is therapeutic; and instead of treating depression, a coach might focus on achieving goals and see if the depression lifts. Failure is therefore *not* something to be avoided or even treated; success is something to be enabled (and by success, I don't necessarily mean relationship success, but any kind of successful experience, such as successful careers, successful management of time, successful approach to money and finances, and so on). This principle, you could say, captures a very Eastern approach to life, and, if you already appreciate this view, you'll find coaching to be very satisfying.

The fourth principle that I discovered is that coaching **is an open paradigm of working with people**. This cannot be undervalued, because this more than anything else is what blazed my coaching trail. Coaching is liberating on many different levels, beyond those that help the person being coached. It also allows you, as a soon-to-be coach, to step outside your routines and zones and approach the mission of helping people in fresh new ways. Coaching *legitimizes* that new approach; it tells you: "Yes, it's okay to do that. It's responsible, it's ethical, it's helpful—and it's necessary." For me, coaching was like learning a new language, one that enabled me to speak to new people in new ways—people I never could have spoken to before. I mean, can you imagine a therapist going out of his or her office to find singles and to try to help them? That's not how it works! As a therapist, I'd have to wait until individuals have suffered so much that their insurance company tells them, "It's okay for you to get *some* therapeutic help." Yet as a coach, I can gloriously walk outside my office, proactively find people who want successful relationships (which pretty much covers everybody), and provide them with safe, ethical, and progressive support to achieve that goal. I can work with functional people who want good relationships. Wow. (Likewise, you can pick a niche or specialty and find mostly healthy people who want to move toward more optimal living in business and/or personal life.)

And the fifth coaching principle that I discovered during my training and put to use in my work is that coaching **affects individuals by empowering them to go after what they want in their lives**. Now, this may not seem like an atom-splitting insight, but there is a subtle point here that resonates very deeply: *Coaching is proactive and intentional*. It's not about diagnosing a client who really has no expertise in whatever they're being diagnosed with. The success or failure of coaching is determined by the client—not by the coach, and not by any tool (e.g., a checklist), strategy, or intervention. As a therapist, even with heartfelt compassion, how many times had I *longed* for clients to take responsibility for their problems—because their failure to do so prevented them from achieving a solution? Coaching doesn't have this problem, because unless clients are using the coaching to go after what they want in their lives, *there is no coaching*. In this way, you could say—and in fact, I'll go ahead and say it—coaching can be more starkly honest than therapy, because if it's not working . . . it's not working. As Forrest Gump might say: *Coaching is as coaching does*. There's nothing to hide behind when it's not working. In fact, when it's not working, it's not coaching.

THE TRANSFORMATION COMPLETES

Probably like you, I worked hard for many years to obtain my clinical license, sacrificing time, money, and quality of life, and my initial intention when I discovered coaching was to practice both as a therapist and as a coach. My identity as a therapist was so strong that the thought of giving it up was shocking—inconceivable, really. Yet as my coaching practice took off, I found that I was having the time of my life creating events for singles, relationship seminars, workshops, classes, and groups, and coaching singles and couples. My work was fun, fulfilling, exciting, profitable, and exhilarating. As my therapy clients dropped off, they were replaced with coaching clients.

And before I knew it, my practice became 100% coaching! While I swore to myself I would *never* give up being a therapist, I found myself referring therapy clients to my colleagues, because, quite simply, coaching was just too much fun, and where I felt I could make the best contribution of my skills.

Yet with all of this being said, I have no regrets about the path I've taken. I believe being a therapist was a long, but effective, road to *becoming* a good coach. Extensive experience with dysfunction gave me a much greater appreciation and understanding of the opportunity to work with functional people. The hardest part of the transition was letting go of judgments and formulas—judgments about what's going on (diagnosis), what intervention (treatment) is needed, what formulas are appropriate based on therapeutic orientation for what box the clients fit in, and what to do with them. Undoing some of my clinical training, but keeping true to the rigorous professional standards and ethics of my license, I feel that I'm now a much more qualified and better coach than someone without a clinical background. As a licensed therapist with a master's degree, I have more credibility with the public, and clients are more willing to hire me knowing I had to jump some pretty high hurdles to earn those initials after my name. You'll likely find this as well: that your background as a therapist supports, rather than interferes with, your reputation and image as a coach.

When asked "What do you do?" my answer is now "I'm a relationship coach." I will always keep and treasure my therapist's license, even though my work no longer requires it. My mission of helping people enjoy successful marriages and stronger families is the same as it always has been, except now I'm doing so in a way that is in much better alignment with who I am, and achieves the results I've always wanted to see for my clients. While I encourage you to continue practicing therapy if you desire, for me, coaching transformed my professional work and identity in ways I never imagined. It simply takes curiosity and an open mind—which you have in abundance already, since you're reading this book and are motivated to make your professional life, and the lives of your clients, better.

Comparing Coaching and Therapy

What is coaching and how is it similar to and different from
  therapy?

How are therapy clients and a therapy practice different from
  coaching clients and a coaching practice?

There are many ways we can dive into this *very* important chapter.
My intention is to introduce you to coaching and provide the perspective needed to decide whether coaching is right for you. We
will cover the "what" of coaching, not the "how." Even so, there's a
lot to cover, and fortunately, all of it is interesting and informative.
In fact, this is probably one of the chapters you'll be referring to
often as you move forward as a coach. So get your pencil and highlighter ready!

We'll start by looking at coaching, and then change gears a little
and discuss some core differences between coaching and therapy.

WHAT IS COACHING?

Coaching can be a confusing term. We coach our kids. We coach our
friends (at least in the informal sense). We watch sports on TV and
see coaches showered with Gatorade. We may even have gone to a

life coach, a nutrition coach, or any other type of coach — even a relationship coach.

So put all that together, and it leads to this: Coaching is something that we obviously need and value as individuals and as a society, but it's hard to say just what it *is* and what it's *not*.

Fortunately, the International Coach Federation (ICF) had the same problem, and so they've defined coaching in the clear terms that follow:

> Coaching is partnering with clients in a thought-provoking and creative process that inspires them to maximize their personal and professional potential. Coaching honors the client as the expert in his/her life and work and believes that every client is creative, resourceful, and whole.

So, both for simplicity and competence (the two tend to go together), I'll be using the ICF's definition throughout this book. And even if I don't explicitly reference it word for word, because that may get in the way of the flow of a particular discussion, I'd encourage you to either memorize the definition or highlight it so you can return to it often. You may even want to write it on one of those ubiquitous yellow sticky notes and place it somewhere handy, like the side of your computer.

So if the preceding tells us, generally, what coaching *is*, we're still left wondering how a coach should function within this definition. Let us wonder no more.

THE COACHING TRIAD: CONCEPTUALIZING AND COMMUNICATING WHAT WE DO

Coaching as an established, standardized profession is the new kid on the block among the helping professions. I've had many prospective clients ask me what I actually do with them in our sessions, confused about the difference between coaching and therapy, and wanting an idea of what to expect.

After many awkward conversations, each explanation different from the one before, I found myself developing and describing The Coaching Triad. There are many ways to conceptualize and describe

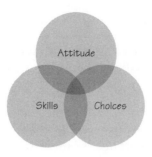

what I do, but I've found The Coaching Triad to be clear, simple, and effective for enrolling prospective clients.

The Coaching Triad typically comes up after the initial discussions about a client's situation and goals. I explain that coaching helps close the gap between where they are and where they want to be, by focusing on the three pillars of **attitude**, **skills**, and **choices**.

Attitudes: Beliefs, Interpretations, Points of View, Stories, Positions, and So On, That Are Acted Out in Behavior

Behavior inevitably follows attitudes. In other words, attitude precedes behavior. Attitudes are influenced by our personality and temperament, family of origin, past experiences, and so on. They can be productive or unproductive, conscious or unconscious. Most important is the fact that we have the power to *choose* our attitudes.

As a coach, you'll see that attitudes show up in how your clients present themselves by what they say, the stories they tell, the explanations they give, and the behaviors they display in session and report occurring outside of session. When I spot an attitude that may be interfering with my clients' goals, I will help them to examine it and perhaps choose a more effective one.

An example of an attitude that I might choose to address is *blaming*, which involves beliefs that put responsibility for the problem and the solution on someone else. I might point out my perception of their attitude, and ask my clients if my perception fits for them, if this attitude has worked so far, and what would be an effective alternative attitude to choose to adopt and practice.

Skills: Learned Habits/Patterns of Adaptive Behavior

Maladaptive habits create barriers to getting what we want, and learning new skills is usually necessary for achieving new goals. These skills are usually learnable and teachable. Most of what we do in life is a pattern of learned behavior that we can modify if we choose to.

Now, I know many therapists are going to complain that this point of view ignores the importance of the emotional realm, for which I have two responses: This is coaching and not therapy, and emotional responses are habitual and are connected to attitudes that can be modified.

A common area for skills training in relationship coaching is conflict resolution, which is often what clients *really mean* when they say they're having "communication problems." In coaching people with this challenge, it's much more important for them to learn the skill of resolving conflict than to focus on the what and the why of their differences with other people. I use the issues that they bring to me as examples in teaching the Communication Map, which I call a "One-Page Communication System for All Relationships" and which is my preferred model for teaching my clients to communicate effectively and resolve issues (http://www.thecommunicationmap.com).

Choices: Decisions Made in the Moment That Result in an Action

We always have a choice. There are no helpless victims in the mature, adult world (notice that this is an *attitude*). Though our choices tend to be the concrete result of our attitudes and skills, we can select our attitudes and skills and can always choose differently. Our choices, large and small, have tremendous long-term consequences and determine our outcomes.

For example, I may be afraid of heights, and may believe anyone would be crazy to jump out of an airplane (attitude). And because I have not done it before and don't know anything about it (skill), I might choose to overcome my fear and do a tandem jump.

"Acting as if" is a common intervention to help people make choices that overcome their limiting attitudes and skills, and is another clear example of exercising choice. Because people always have a choice, your job as coach is to help your clients make effective choices to help them get what they want in their lives and relationships.

A COACH'S RESPONSIBILITY IN THE CLIENT-COACH PARTNERSHIP

The first thing you'll want to note is that, again, we're calling it a *partnership* and not a *relationship*. This is not semantics. Although a partnership is a relationship, a relationship is not necessarily a partnership.

As a coach, you are *partnering* with your client in the most literal sense of the word. Yes, you know more about your area of expertise. That's fine and the way it's supposed to be. But you don't know more about your client than he or she does. And so coaching works only when both parties form a genuine partnership built on mutual sharing, collaboration, and cooperation. This is of particular importance, and sometimes difficult for therapists to tolerate (grasping it is easy; doing it is quite another thing).

For a therapist and a client, the relationship—not the partnership—is fundamentally asymmetrical. It's one-sided, similar to the relationship between a doctor and a patient. And there's nothing at all *wrong* with that—as long as it's therapy.

But when it changes to coaching, the framework has to change, too. It's no longer asymmetrical; it's even. And the only way for both parties to achieve what they want to achieve from the coaching (the client: to be helped; the coach: to help) is for each to humbly accept and respect the value and autonomy of the other. If either party is unwilling or incapable of doing this, the coaching *can't* happen. And when it doesn't happen, never think that it's the fault of the coaching. The coaching is fine. It's the people *doing it* that have to adjust, and until they do, it won't work.

So with that said, what do professional coaches do all day? They provide an ongoing partnership that helps their clients produce fulfilling results in their personal and professional lives. Ultimately, coaches help people improve their performances and enhance the quality of their lives.

And how do they do it? Coaches are trained to listen, to observe, and to customize their approach to individual client needs. They seek to elicit solutions and strategies from the client; they believe the client is naturally creative and resourceful. The coach's job is to provide support to enhance the skills, resources, and creativity that the client already has.

In short, coaches:

- discover, clarify, and align with what the client wants to achieve;
- encourage client self-discovery;
- elicit client-generated solutions and strategies; and
- hold the client responsible and accountable for actions and results.

BASIC COACHING SKILLS

As a coach, you'll no doubt rely on many of the skills and strengths you've cultivated as a therapist: namely, your ability to use your intuition, listen carefully, and focus on your client's needs.

However, the coach's tool kit is somewhat less technical than the therapist's. This doesn't mean that it's inferior or weaker. It's simply a different approach and emphasis. As a therapist you might need to know a lot about a problem—what causes it, strategies for treating it, and so forth. As a coach, believe it or not, you don't need to be an expert in the subject that is the focus of the coaching; you just need to apply your coaching skills expertly. For example, you don't need to know how to build a house to coach a building contractor who wants to build better houses. Your clients will teach you everything you need to know about their problem and solution as you are coaching them.

Here are 12 basic coaching skills that you'll use and reuse in your practice, some of which you might recognize that you already use with your clients:

1. **Accentuating the positive**—highlighting strengths, cheerleading accomplishments, and helping your client stay optimistic and focused on goals and solutions.
2. **Accountability**—obtaining commitment to action items that your client chooses, and accounting for the results.

3. **Challenging**—requesting that your clients stretch beyond their self-imposed limits.
4. **Clarifying**—questioning, reframing, and articulating what's going on.
5. **Designing the alliance**—assisting your clients to take responsibility by deciding the form of support most beneficial to them. In therapy, the therapist usually designs the alliance, whereas in coaching the client does.
6. **Forwarding the action**—using a variety of skills to move clients a step forward toward their goal.
7. **Holding the client's agenda**—probably the most important and distinctive coaching skill. As a coach, you become almost invisible and without judgment, opinion, or answers, which allows your client to access his or her own answers.
8. **Holding the focus**—assisting your client to keep on track when distracted by feelings, circumstances, and so on.
9. **Maintaining an attitude of inquiry**—being curious, supportive, positive, and nonjudgmental.
10. **Powerful questions**—asking open-ended questions that evoke clarity, deepen learning, and propel action.
11. **Reflective listening**—providing a mirror to help your client increase insight, understanding, and clarity.
12. **Requesting**—forwarding the action by making a request based on your client's agenda.

COACHING GUIDELINES

The goal of coaching is to empower clients, *not* to prescribe or advise as an expert. Again, this is an area where therapists may struggle as coaches because they're so used to being the source of knowledge and interventions; that is what their clients (and insurance billing requirements) have expected of them.

Coaching, however, requires a different paradigm: one where the information flows from the *bottom up* rather than from the *top down*. That is, an effective coach supports, emphasizes, and encourages the latent or neglected strengths of a client. He or she does not "diagnose and treat." (Oh, and by the way, if you're a fee-for-service therapist who doesn't diagnose, *no*, that doesn't make you a coach; it simply makes you a fee-for-service therapist who doesn't diagnose.)

The art of coaching involves facilitating learning while holding our clients as the experts on their lives and what works for them. Here are some guidelines to help conceptualize the role of the coach and client in coaching:

- **Coaching is not consulting or therapy.**

  Coaching empowers by assuming your client is the expert who is capable of achieving goals. Your job is to support action. Consulting typically provides advice and solutions, whereas therapy typically focuses on insight and resolution of emotional issues. Because these approaches are so different, as a coach you should be clear about these distinctions, educate your client about them, and make choices about the nature of the coaching relationship that are in the best interests of your client.

- **A coach helps clients focus on the bigger picture.**

  Coaching is not effective when isolating your clients' goals from the rest of their lives, such as work, family, friends, wellness, spirituality, and so on.

- **A coach shares knowledge, experience, and information without attachment.**

  Sharing expertise and information with your clients as a coach is very different from any other type of helping relationship. It's necessary to address your clients' skills and knowledge deficits; however, you should do so in a way that supports them to discover and own their truths.

- **A coach assumes a goal is part of the journey, not the destination.**

  You support your clients to focus on meaning, connection, living a balanced life, and working toward long-term goals.

- **A coach assumes that the most important relationship is the one you have with yourself.**

  The Law of Attraction dictates that "like attracts like" and that what is inside shows up on the outside. You want to help your clients set goals in alignment with their values, make choices in alignment with their goals, take responsibility for their outcomes, and allow themselves to be authentically who they are (because they can't be anyone else!).

- **A coach does not judge right or wrong, good or bad.**

  Your clients are the experts on themselves, and as a coach you must honor their truths and agendas. Although you may have judgments, you don't impose them on your clients. Rather, you lead your clients along a process of discovery through which they are empowered to make the choices that are right for them.

- **A coach does not seek to get personal needs met with clients or prospective clients.**

  An ethical coach values being of service above all else, holds the coaching relationship sacred, and doesn't allow a personal agenda to interfere with this commitment.

- **A coach addresses clients' sabotaging attitudes and choices without making them wrong.**

  Assume that attitude precedes outcome, and skillfully help your clients become aware of how attitudes (beliefs, interpretations, etc.), choices, and consequences are connected. You support your clients in making their own judgments and decisions about their choices in alignment with their visions, purposes, requirements, needs, and goals. You may internally disagree and judge your clients wrong, but you don't impose your judgment upon them.

- **A coach is neutral about the outcome for the client.**

  You shouldn't be attached to any particular outcome. Instead, you should acknowledge that your clients are in charge of their lives, choices, and outcomes. As a coach, you work hard to support your clients, but you don't work harder than they do. You need to hold your clients accountable for their actions and results.

- **A coach walks the talk by continually addressing his or her own personal development, challenges, and goals.**

  You can only help your clients along paths that you have traveled yourself—and no further. So you must continually strive to be conscious and intentional in your life and relationships. This includes furthering your own learning and development by working with a coach or mentor, ongoing training, and other means. How can we expect prospective clients to hire us for coaching if we don't walk our talk and work with a coach ourselves? Look at it this way: *Investing in yourself will help your prospective clients see the value of investing in working with you.*

- **A coach uses self-disclosure to diminish professional distance.**

    Most therapists are trained to *severely* limit self-disclosure, because it detracts from focusing on the client. Coaching turns that approach on its head! In coaching, self-disclosure is used to *bridge* the gap between coach and client. It helps establish rapport, empathy, compassion, and trust. It also forces—yes, I said *forces*—a coach to be an authentic, real person, not an expert who can hide behind jargon, degrees, or the other trappings that tend to function (ironically) as blocks rather than bridges. The thing is—and this is going to be hard for some therapists to digest—a coach *wants* to be viewed by clients as a normal human being—that is, someone who is flawed and who has good days, bad days, hopes, regrets, and all of the other things that make us beautifully, tragically human. When this view is established, clients can relate to their coach and real communication happens. It opens the door to change and improvement.

How Is Coaching Similar to Therapy? How Is It Different?

Inevitably, we've already covered some of this territory, because it helps put the concepts and fundamentals of coaching into sharper relief when it can be compared to something you know quite well—which is your role as a therapist.

However, it's worth focusing specifically on coaching/therapy similarities and differences, because doing so will not only help you define what it is you do, but it will just as valuably help you communicate your role to clients and allied professionals. Indeed, chances are you'll be asked now and then, "So why aren't you a therapist?" or you'll hear the comment, "That sounds like therapy." This section helps you easily answer these questions in terms that anyone can understand and appreciate.

Warning: What follows are generalities that are not meant to definitively cover every iteration and variation of coaching or therapy. Prepare to disagree! Consider the next sections to be for guideline purposes only.

Let's start by looking at the similarities between coaching and therapy. This is *not* intended to be a complete list (because such a thing is not possible); however, these are the basics, the pillars. I hope you'll find these similarities satisfying and, indeed, inspiring, because they help you more clearly understand that you *do not* sacrifice the core goals of being a devoted, dedicated, and qualified helping professional when you transition from therapist to coach.

Similarities between the role of a coach and that of a therapist include:

- An ongoing, confidential, one-to-one, fee-for-service relationship
- Working with clients who want to change
- Assuming change occurs only over time
- Use of verbal dialogue as the primary service activity
- Regularly scheduled sessions

See Table 2.1 for some *differences* between the role of a coach and that of a therapist.

And to expand this view even further, see Tables 2.2, 2.3, and 2.4 for some handy compilations that point out other differences.

I realize that these comparisons are generalizations and there are exceptions and differences of opinion. This information is for exploring the differences between coaching and therapy and is not intended to be definitive.

Table 2.1 Differences between Coaches and Therapists

Therapy	Coaching
Assumes the client needs healing.	Assumes the client is whole.
Roots are in medicine, psychiatry.	Roots are in sports, business, personal growth venues.
Works with people to achieve self-understanding and emotional healing.	Works to move people to a higher level of functioning.
Focuses on feelings and past events.	Focuses on actions and the future.
Explores the root of problems.	Focuses on solving problems.
Works to bring the unconscious into consciousness.	Works with the conscious mind.
Works for internal resolution of pain and to let go of old patterns.	Works for external solutions to overcome barriers, learn new skills, and implement effective choices.

22

Table 2.2 Comparing Five Types of Helping Professionals

Type and definition	License required?	Degree required?	Primary income source	Focus of service	Who's the expert?	Prescribe solutions?
Therapists: licensed clinical professionals trained to diagnose and treat mental and emotional disorders	Yes	Yes	Insurance, private pay, employer	Problems, insight, healing, growth	Therapist	Yes
Counselors: provide guidance to help a person resolve social or personal problems	Yes, for LPC, no for others	Yes, for LPC, no for others	Employer	Problems, insight, functioning	Counselor	Yes
Educators: teach or instruct a person or group for some particular purpose or occupation	No	Yes	Employer	Learning	Educator	Yes
Consultants: specialists who give expert advice or information to solve problems and optimize functioning	No	No	Employer	Problems	Consultant	Yes
Coaches: help their clients identify and achieve their goals, assuming the client is the expert.	No	No	Private pay, employer	Goals	Client	No

Table 2.3 *Comparing Therapy and Coaching Clients*

	What typically motivates clients?	How do clients typically perceive themselves?	What do clients typically want?	How do clients typically interact with the helping professional?
Therapy	Pain	Feel that something is wrong with them. Tend to feel bad about needing therapy.	An end to struggles in an important area of their life (money, relationships, work, legal, etc.).	Are not fully functional, often tell stories to explain their problems and want the therapist to fix them. Sometimes argue, resist suggestions, and question the effectiveness of your help.
Coaching	Goal achievement	Empowering themselves by engaging extra support to ensure success and tend to feel good about themselves for hiring a coach.	Focus positively on their goals, and are motivated to improve and advance.	Take ownership of their outcomes, are functional, supportable, open-minded, and action-oriented.

Table 2.4 Comparing the Business of Therapy and Coaching

	Fee Schedule	Billing	Liability	Service Delivery	Getting Clients
Therapy	Usually charge by the session after the service is rendered.	Often bill insurance.	Provide clinical treatment and deal with their client's deepest vulnerabilities and are required to have liability insurance in most settings.	Almost always delivered in person in an office, usually 1:1 but can be in groups. The therapist determines the what, when, where, and how of therapy.	Most therapy clients self-refer or are referred by another professional. Most therapy clients will want their medical insurance to pay, if eligible, influencing their selection of therapist and treatment modality. The pool of people who qualify and identify that they need therapy is finite.
Coaching	Usually charge by the month in advance.	Accept only private pay (cash, check, or credit card).	Insurance is optional for coaches, and many choose not to carry liability insurance as they are not responsible for their clients' outcomes and have their clients sign a contract to this effect.	Coaching can be in person, over the telephone, online, pretty much anywhere. The coach designs the alliance with the client, and the location, frequency, and other variables can be tailored to the client. A coach is more likely to integrate multiple services and revenue streams into the practice, such as workshops, seminars, classes, retreats, groups, and other creative service modalities.	The pool of possible coaching clients is far larger, almost infinite; however, there are no ready-made coaching clients referred by their physicians and funded by their insurance companies. Coaching clients tend to be created through the efforts of the coach; therefore, coaches need to be more entrepreneurial and proactive in their marketing and enrollment.

What general conclusions can we take away from these similarities and differences?

- All helping professionals care deeply about people and want to make a positive difference in their lives and the world.
- Coaching is the only profession that doesn't assume the expert role and impose judgments or prescriptions on the client/patient/student.
- The self-perception of all the helping professions (except coaching) is that the professional is the expert and the client needs the expert's professional opinions.
- The self-perception of a client working with all the helping professionals (except coaches) is that the professional knows more than the client, who should listen and do what the professional says.
- Helping professionals typically focus on their *service* (such as cognitive-behavioral therapy, marriage counseling, etc.) and accept just about any client appropriate for their service or scope of practice. A coach, in contrast, focuses on the *client* and his or her outcomes and will typically be selective and work with only certain kinds of clients.

TELEPHONE VERSUS IN PERSON

Therapists work almost exclusively in person with their clients, and it shouldn't be any other way. Even with the increasing acceptance of therapy by telephone and the Internet, I don't believe therapy can be delivered effectively outside an office, even via video chat.

Coaching, by contrast, can be delivered in person or over the telephone. In fact, I've discovered that coaching is more effectively delivered over the phone. Here's why telephone coaching works:

- It's more convenient for coach and client.
- It decreases the likelihood of a client canceling due to traveling.
- It cuts down on late appointments.
- It allows you to have shorter sessions—it's *amazing* how much you can accomplish in a 30-minute phone call.

- It makes it easier to focus on actions and results—the telephone seems more conducive to getting down to business and staying focused on that business than meeting in person.
- It makes it easier to focus on the client—the telephone seems to facilitate the coach's being "invisible" (described later in this chapter).
- It compels you, the coach, to listen more, without depending on body language and visual cues; your listening skills become sharper, and your intuition does, too.

You don't, of course, have to provide *only* telephone coaching. You can combine it with in-person coaching. For example, you can meet once per month in person (for an hour, or even a whole day or weekend), and supplement it with telephone check-ins and sessions.

However, if you simply don't want to coach over the telephone, don't worry: You don't have to! It's not a requirement (though you won't get the advantages I've noted). Perhaps the challenge is, simply, that you've never worked with a client over the phone and aren't sure how to proceed. If that's the case, then an easy way to get started is to establish a "buddy coaching" relationship with a fellow trainee from your coach training program. This is one of the best ways to practice your coaching skills, to experience coaching, and to become more comfortable using the telephone as your coaching tool.

Bonus tip: If you're going to use the telephone for your training or coaching, get a comfortable headset!

How Do You Know If a Client Is Right for Coaching or Therapy?

Most coach training programs advise: "When in doubt, refer it out." This is a handy guideline, but things get more complex when any of these issues crop up:

- A client insists on coaching and won't even consider therapy.
- The coach is also a therapist and is able to address therapeutic issues.

- The individual or couple is in therapy, or has tried therapy, and wants coaching.
- The therapist/coach sees the value of therapy, but also identifies that the client is functional and a solid candidate for coaching.

Any or all of these issues create a screening challenge that simply doesn't exist (to such an extent) in therapy. As a coach, you need to screen for coachability before accepting a client.

SCREENING FOR COACHABILITY

With experience, you'll be able to educate your prospective clients so that you won't have to do all of the screening; your clients will, thanks to your explanation of the promises and limitations of coaching, easily self-identify that they are or aren't good candidates to receive coaching.

Be aware that some clients want your help with their problem or goal and don't care what you call the service. It's probably unnecessary to ask, "Do you want therapy or coaching?" The prospective client probably doesn't have enough information to answer that question. I suggest you ask the person's reasons for contacting you, do your usual assessment and intake, use your best judgment to decide how best to proceed, and then let the person know what you recommend and why.

Until then, however, here are some tips to keep you on the right path:

o **Pick and choose your clients.** This can be challenging when you're starting out, because sending away potential clients doesn't seem like a smart business strategy. But remember, your goal is to help, and there are some prospective clients who really aren't suitable for coaching. So basically, if you see a red flag (or more likely, a sea of red flags) and the little voice inside you *knows* that you're just taking the client to pay the bills, snap out of your trance and reread this chapter.

o **Get more information.** Sometimes, you won't have a definitive "coach/don't coach" answer when considering taking on a new client. In such cases, partner with the individuals and encourage them to seek assessment by another helping professional, such as a physician or psychologist. Coaching may ultimately be the right path for them, but that determination will need to take place down the road.

o **Reverse diagnosis.** In some situations, you are confident that potential clients are *not* in need of other helping modalities (e.g., therapy), but you aren't sure whether coaching will help them achieve their goals. This is because, as I've stressed throughout this book (and have no intentions of stopping!), whether coaching truly works or doesn't depends extensively on the client, not the coach. In such situations, reverse diagnosis can provide you with the confirmation you need. For example, you might contract with clients for 30 to 90 days of coaching. If they improve their functioning thanks to coaching, then voilà—they're coachable!

o **Regularly check level of functioning.** If you're concerned about your clients' need for therapy, but they objectively benefit from your coaching, then keep tabs on their functioning by regularly checking to see if there are any adverse issues with sleeping, eating, self-care, moods, relationships, work productivity, and so on. Of course, ensure that you clearly explain to your clients *why* you're doing this. And if they report any impaired functioning, coach them to set a goal, strategize, and implement an action plan to address their issues, which may include medical or psychiatric assistance.

o **Establish conditions for coaching.** If your client is also seeking therapy (and remember—do not provide therapy and coaching to the same client at the same time!), then, in your contract, make that individual commit to addressing therapeutic issues with a therapist.

o **Identify high stress.** Here's an unusual but surprisingly effective technique: When prospective clients call you, pay careful attention to their voice mail. If you hear high stress, desperation, and/or depression in their voices, they *usually* are not coachable and need therapy. Or, if you hear functionality, that *same* functionality will usually be present when you follow up with them.

o **Have an agreement.** Create a small agreement with your clients that will require them to e-mail or leave you a voice mail three times over the next week after they have exercised (or meditated, or updated their checkbook, or whatever small goal they might have). Good coaching clients will be more likely to follow through, knowing that they'll be held accountable, whereas a therapy client will be much less likely to follow through, having bigger internal obstacles to functioning and self-direction.

EARLY EXPERIENCE WITH REVERSE DIAGNOSIS

Early in my coaching career, a prospective client informed me that he had for years been in extensive therapy for anxiety and depression and felt stuck. The therapy wasn't helping him, and he needed something else: coaching.

Naturally, I expressed reservations because he wasn't a highly functioning individual and coaching works with functional people. However, he pleaded for me to coach him, so I agreed to give it a try—but I implemented the reverse diagnosis screening technique described earlier. We agreed to a 30-day coaching trial, set goals and action plans, and met weekly for a month.

It didn't work. Each week, despite my efforts to redirect him and focus on his goals, he would start the session with his latest dramatic event and ask the same three questions over and over: "Why does this happen to me?" "Why do I do this?" "What should I do?" He wasn't able to follow through with a *single* agreement or action plan. At the end of the month, I explained he wasn't ready for coaching and referred him back to his therapist. The coaching, although not doing any harm, could not penetrate his clinical symptoms.

However, I've had other clients since then who were just as frustrated as this client, and within the first few weeks of coaching they turned their lives around and became excited and empowered—which *wouldn't* have happened if I'd started with a therapy approach to address their depression. As you can see, reverse diagnosis can be a very effective way to determine coachability, but must be used with good judgment.

WHAT DOES COACHING LOOK LIKE?
TOM'S BREAKTHROUGH

To help you see what coaching with a coachable client looks like, let me share an experience I had with a client named Tom (not his real name).

Tom was a middle-aged, never-married single entrepreneur who really wanted to find his life partner, so he signed up for my Conscious Dating® coaching program for singles. Through my program, Tom became clear about his vision for his life, relationship requirements, needs, and wants. Together, we developed a relationship plan of goals and action steps for achieving that vision.

One of Tom's action steps was to contact at least five women per week through an Internet dating website. We started working on his business goals as well, and each week we met and reviewed his progress.

After a few months, I noticed that Tom had not contacted any new dating prospects, and I asked him why. His response was, "I don't think anyone would want to date me right now because my business isn't making any money yet." I was shocked. I had no idea he held this limiting belief, but his lack of dating progress started to make sense. I reflected on this, and presented him with a simple but *powerful* question: "Do you want to be loved for who you are, or for how much money you make?"

Tom fell silent. And in coaching, when a client is silent in response to a coaching question, it often means you've hit a home run. In other words, the question has penetrated through the client's layers of personality and limiting defense mechanisms, and has resonated within the deepest core of being where the client's truth is, simply, the truth.

After a few moments of this celebrated silence, Tom responded passionately, "I want to be loved for who I am!"

Now, before we go into how this changed Tom's action plan, it's immensely valuable to pay close attention to the fact that it was *Tom* who discovered this truth within himself, and for himself. Yes, without doubt, I had hoped he would answer my question that way. But nevertheless, it wasn't for me—as his coach—to prescribe the right answer for him, and then explain (or maybe even not explain) why it was right. That's not how coaching works. As a coach, you create situations and contexts for your clients to discover *their* truths, and it's within that discovery process that change takes place. In the simplest terms: I didn't have to talk Tom into believing the truth of his statement, and further, there was no chance that later that day or next week or next year he would ever feel that he was persuaded into believing something that wasn't ultimately true for him. When clients discover their truth within, it's strong and confident—even if the truth may be scary and challenging.

In a way, you could say that finding that truth is like spotting a mountain. The mountain can be small, medium, large, or Himalayan. And climbing that mountain, whatever the size, will naturally present challenges. But *seeing* the mountain—seeing the truth of it, its shape, its reality— must happen first. And when coaching clients *see* their mountain, they can take intelligent steps to climb it. And that's what Tom did!

So, thanks to Tom and to coaching, we reframed his situation. Instead of this being a scary and undesirable time to date, it became the *ideal* time because he had little risk of attracting a woman more interested in his money than in him. In fact, he might even find someone supportive who could play a role, or be a partner, in his business— which was an important part of his vision.

This coaching-inspired epiphany broke the dam, and in the ensuing months, Tom met many women whom he otherwise would never even have thought of approaching, let alone dating. And in that process—as he climbed his inner mountain—he learned to enjoy the journey and adventure of meeting new people, while never losing faith that he would eventually find the love of his life. His confidence soared, and his business did, too!

Okay: Let's back up and imagine that Tom had seen a therapist instead of a coach. A therapist might view Tom as having low self-esteem and not being ready for dating. The target, then, would have been Tom's self-esteem, and that could (and would) have taken *months* to deal with. Hours upon hours would be spent exploring Tom's past, identifying seminal events that shaped his self-image, and so on. By the time Tom was beyond his self-esteem issues—or at least enough so that he could take productive, positive action and address his dating challenges— invaluable time would have passed, and so would have opportunity.

Now, let's openly admit there *are* some challenges in life for which the coaching process is not appropriate. Sometimes the issues are severe and pathological (e.g., psychotic behavior, suicidal ideation, etc.). Coaches don't go *near* clients with these issues, because that's what other helping professions—like psychotherapy—are for.

Resolving those kinds of issues, if they can ever truly be resolved, can take *years*.

But Tom clearly wasn't in that situation, so to apply the standard therapist "diagnose and treat" model to him would have been haphazard and potentially damaging if it cost him the chance to seize current opportunities and make the best use of his time *and* money. Instead, coaching was ideal. It helped him take focused action that was based on clear, inner understanding. It helped him move forward because *that's what he wanted to do.*

Of course, if we hadn't been successful after a while, I would have referred him for therapy and opened up the conversation about whether he was ready for a relationship. However, I would *not* have imposed that as my "professional opinion."

BEING "INVISIBLE"

One of the striking differences between coaching and other helping professions is the element of being transparent or invisible. This is more of an art than a science.

Being invisible refers to a coach's ability to shine the light of attention and encouragement upon her or his client, without inserting opinion or invading the client's sacred space. Personally, I've found my being invisible to be incredibly empowering to my clients, and the best way to support them to be the true experts and sources of their solutions.

Now, one of the chief misunderstandings about being invisible — and we'll chalk this one up to the limitations of language — is that being invisible does not mean that you, as a coach, are not participating or that you are somehow turned off and tuned out of the situation. On the contrary, by suspending judgment and simply enabling your clients to get in touch with their internal truth, you are actively cocreating the experience with them; you're simply doing it in a graceful, empowering way. Instead of going up to the mountain and pulling your clients to the peak, you're gently supporting them as they make the ascent themselves — slowly or quickly, methodically or sporadically; it's up to them. It's *their* climb, after all.

Furthermore, don't perceive that by being invisible you must become silent and inert. Often, you can helpfully influence the situation by *how* you say things. For example, you may help your client reframe a situation by asking a question that invites him or her to see it in a new light. In this way, you are still invisible — because you are not dictating or prescribing or diagnosing — yet you are helping.

Even though a coach doesn't give advice, it is still possible to insert your agenda through leading questions, such as the one I asked Tom: "Do you want to be loved for who you are, or for how much money you make?" It's a great coaching question, but if my goal had been to be invisible I could have asked, "How true is that?" or responded with a similar question to his statement, "I don't think anyone would want to date me right now because my business isn't making any money yet." It requires judgment when and how to insert information or an opinion in a "coach-like" manner, and the goal is always to empower the client without attachment.

CAN COACHING DO HARM?

It's an important question to ask — and the fact that I'm asking it near the end of the chapter is not to diminish that importance; rather, it's to make it all that much easier for you to refer to it as you develop as a coach.

In my opinion, by itself coaching is harmless. In my experience, however, there are three ways a coach can harm a client:

1. Unskilled coaching: giving advice, imposing judgment, prescribing interventions, doing therapy while calling it coaching, mixing coaching and therapy, and other activities that actually are *not* coaching.
2. Continuing ineffective coaching.
3. Providing coaching instead of what's really needed, such as therapy, psychiatric intervention, and so forth.

As you can see, there is nothing earth-shattering or esoteric about this. It's common sense, and if you've been practicing for some time as a therapist, these guiding principles are second nature to you. Basically, you need to be competent, be realistic, and use good professional judgment.

DUAL RELATIONSHIPS: JUST SAY NO

Therapists are usually prohibited from entering into dual relationships with their clients, such as becoming socially or romantically involved, entering business ventures, or even bartering. These dual relationships also cover conflicts of interest, such as coaching friends, family members, business associates, and so on. Being a coach and a therapist to the same client at the same time is also a form of dual relationship. As a therapist, having more than one relationship with your client risks the effectiveness of your therapy, and can potentially damage the client. It can also potentially create a litigious situation for you. As a coach, I highly recommend that you adopt the therapist's "no dual relationships" boundary and standard.

SOME FINAL THOUGHTS

Having had extensive experience in both therapy and coaching, I've arrived at the opinion that we *disempower* clients by assuming they know less about themselves than we do. Further, clients—unintentionally—*disempower* themselves when they accept this power imbalance.

The simple truth I've realized through and with coaching is that people support what they help create. If you agree with the wisdom of this, you must also see, logically, that prescribing solutions rarely works when a collaborative coaching partnership is an appropriate option.

Also, having worked for many years in nonprofit agencies and in private practice (insurance billing) where clients pay little or nothing out of pocket, I've realized that when a helping service requires significant client follow-through, those same clients tend to benefit *more* from a service they invest in. In other words, the results are tied, subtly and perhaps unconsciously, to how clients participate in and cocreate their improved results. The moral to this story? Asking clients to pay for their coaching is neither evil nor prohibitive. In fact, it can be downright beneficial!

Ultimately, when you take in everything I've covered—and you may need to read the chapter a few times to really grasp all of the details—I hope you'll arrive at the fundamental fact that the practice and business of therapy and coaching are very different.

But that begs the question: Is "very different" good . . . or bad? That is a question that I won't answer, simply because it's not for me to do that. It's for you. Only you can decide if being a coach is right for you, and if it enables you to access and experience many of the things you want to have in your professional life. In other words, you may have thought that being a therapist was the only path that your career could travel. If nothing else, I'd like to think this chapter has given you a solid, credible, and objective reason to question that assumption.

The remaining chapters will now focus on how to take your attraction or open-mindedness to coaching and integrate it or transition it into your practice.

CHAPTER THREE

How to Become a Coach

Do you need coaching training?
How do you find training that doesn't duplicate what you
  already know?
How can you be a coach *and* a therapist?

Do You Need Coaching Training?

By now, you can safely guess that my answer to this question will be
a definitive *yes*. Yet your answer may not be as unwavering, particularly if you discuss the issue with colleagues, peers, or just your next-
door neighbor, all of whom may suggest in their well-intentioned but
gloriously wrong view that training is optional. Or worse, some of
the more enthusiastically misled among them may go as far as to tell
you that as a therapist you already know how to coach, so coaching
training is unnecessary. Reading a book, or even being a therapist,
doesn't mean you know how to coach.

Let's clear up this view once and for all. Coaching training is not
merely necessary; it's mandatory. Repeat: mandatory. (Please keep
repeating until memorized; yes, there *will* be an exam in the form of
how satisfying and lucrative your budding coaching career will—or
won't—be.)

Coaching training isn't mandatory in the legal sense, but mandatory so you really know what coaching is and learn how to do it, as
opposed to just saying you are a coach.

And here's why it's mandatory: Coaching is (for the time being) an unregulated profession, and as such, technically, anyone can call himself or herself a coach. However, unregulated is not synonymous with unprofessional. On the contrary, coaching is a profession. A profession is commonly defined as *an occupation requiring specialized education and/or training*. Therefore, a professional coach is someone who has specialized education and/or training in coaching.

It's really that simple. And, it's also simple to overlook or never grasp in the first place. Indeed, coaching can be misunderstood by other helping professionals, because (as we discussed in Chapter 2) it's different from therapy, counseling, consulting, and education—and yet many professionals in these fields either call themselves "coach" or claim to be "coaching." For example, a sex therapist might call himself a "sex coach," a nutritionist might call herself a "wellness coach," a business consultant might call himself a "business coach," a financial planner or investment adviser might call herself a "financial coach," a family lawyer or mediator might call himself a "divorce coach," and so on. As a therapist, in a well-intentioned effort to be efficient, you may be tempted to read this book, believe that you understand the ins and outs of coaching, and start to market your coaching services. Let me be very clear on this point: To do so is both wrong and a mistake. Don't do it.

Now, the last thing I want you to infer from this discussion is that I'm one of those professional coaches who go around waving their fists in the air, decrying how many people from all walks of life are calling themselves coaches. Okay, though this *is* irritating, it doesn't have to do with market share or competition. I'm not (at all) worried that these pseudo-coaches are going to take revenue out of my practice. The frustration here is not about self-interest or self-preservation; it's about something much, much bigger than me.

Why Coaching Training and Coaching *Professionals* Matter

I love coaching and coaches, and I've dedicated my life to this field and to this craft. And, frankly, what some unprofessional coaches (i.e., untrained people calling themselves coaches) are doing is a violation of the ethics, standards, morals, and sometimes even the laws that all professionals—not just professional coaches, but *all* professionals in *all* fields—strive to uphold. After all, these are the very things that separate the professional from the unprofessional.

Yet, without going on a rant, there are self-described coaches claiming to be professionals, but who lack training. As such, they simply aren't professionals. And that's a problem.

Why? Glad you asked. In my experience there are four primary types of damage that noncoaches inflict on their clients and the coaching profession as a whole.

1. **Untrained coaches damage the coaching profession by creating confusion about coaching.**

   They don't understand the intent or—and this is extremely important—the *limitations* of coaching. Indeed, as much as I love coaching, I fail to advance the profession if my vision becomes cloudy and I start to make broad, sweeping claims about what coaching can do. Coaching is but one approach to helping; it *doesn't* replace other legitimate helping professions such as therapy, counseling, and more. Unfortunately, many unprofessional coaches (who aren't even coaches at all) have no grasp of this reality. They make ridiculous, irresponsible, and sometimes even *illegal* claims about what coaching is able to do.

2. **Untrained coaches damage their clients by behaviors that are *not* coaching and do not serve the clients' best interests.**

   They give advice, provide supposedly professional opinions, and call it coaching, but they impose their so-called wisdom on their unwitting clients instead of supporting the clients to discover their own wisdom.

   Pseudo-coaches often do more than just confuse their clients; they offer unsubstantiated or just plain incompetent opinions and advice that can be destructive. The consequences of this are far-reaching but not difficult to evaluate: The clients' best interests are not served. They don't get the *coaching* they need.

3. **Untrained coaches damage the reputation of coaching itself.**

   Most unprofessional (and untrained) coaches are dabbling in coaching; they're trying it out because it looks like a popular, (dare I say it) easy way to make money. However, when they fail to help their clients or, more likely, when they make things worse for their clients, they also erode the credibility of real, professional coaches and coaching. Why? Because the unprofessional coach's victims (they're no longer clients at this point, but *victims*) are, naturally, going to tell everyone they know to never trust this coaching stuff. (They'll likely call it something else, but I have to say "stuff" because this is a professional book.)

4. **Untrained coaches harm themselves because they tend to wash out fairly quickly as word spreads about them and they can't get clients.**

   Though I reserve no compassion for unprofessional coaches who knowingly deceive or cut corners in order to cash in on coaching's growing appeal, I'll admit that there are some unprofessional coaches who simply don't know that training must be part of their professional makeup. Perhaps they were misled by another unprofessional coach. Yet regardless of what led them to this stage, the fact is that they, ironically, will be their own worst enemy because their reputation won't grow. Actually, it *will* grow—just in the wrong direction. Indeed, though there are many great marketing strategies for reaching new clients, word-of-mouth marketing in its myriad of forms (including social networking) is always going to be a staple of a coaching practice's success . . . or a core reason for its failure.

   Unprofessional, untrained coaches who are armed with (we can optimistically hope) nothing more than good intentions are doomed. And yes, while I have compassion for this breed of coaches, I can't say I shed a tear when I see them exit the field.

MOST OF 'EM ARE GOOD PEOPLE, BUT . . .

Most unprofessional coaches that I've encountered have good intentions. Yes, they're motivated by money, but they want to help, too!
And yet they truly have no idea they're behaving unprofessionally
and unethically. They often believe that their life experiences qualify
them to help others in similar situations. They don't understand that
merely reading books, listening to CDs, purchasing home study programs, attending workshops, or even having a college degree doesn't
qualify them or give them the skills they need to competently help
others with their most important life goals and challenges.

My friend Patrick Williams, EdD (coaching pioneer and founder of
the Institute for Life Coach Training), says, "In the early years of coaching I coached as a psychologist and also coached top-level executives,
but when the coaching profession evolved and developed a coach-
specific knowledge base of skills, techniques, and strategies, I learned
new approaches and became an even better coach. Today, coach-specific
training from a reputable training program is essential for your success."

"BUT I DON'T NEED COACHING
TRAINING BECAUSE . . ."

As a licensed therapist, there's a possibility that this whole idea of
getting trained as a coach is, well, *annoying* is the nicest way to put it.
Why? Because here I am telling you that you need coaching training
before calling yourself a coach, yet there are many untrained people
out there claiming to be coaches. And to make things worse, those
same untrained people are encroaching on your territory, claiming to
do all the things that you do with your clients. Put all this together
and the notion that you should be trained as a coach before adding
that title to your business card can be hard to digest. Believe me
when I say that I understand and sympathize.

In response to this, I'll drum up a quote from Gerald Celente (pub-
lisher of the *Trends Journal*), which gets to the heart of the matter:
"Opportunity misses those who view the world only through the eyes

of their professions." And if we rephrase this for our context (I'm sure Gerald won't mind), we can say: "If you view the world only through the eyes of a therapist, you're resisting reality."

And what *is* that reality? It's twofold:

First, coaching is a legitimate profession that requires specific education and training (which is the definition of *profession*).

So, if you think you already know how to coach, then guess what? By definition, you *don't* and *can't*. Your very argument *proves* that you need training.

Or if that isn't persuasive enough, try this: How would you react if, say, a hairstylist with a reputation for giving advice began pitching her services as a coach? Better yet, as a coach in your area of specialization — say, helping women with eating disorders as a "body image coach." Your reaction would be a combination of disbelief, horror, and anger. Obviously, you'd demand that this hairstylist/coach go through *some* form of training before claiming the job title. And the same applies to you. Yes, your work as a therapist can certainly help you as a coach. Without question, my background as a therapist has supported me in many ways. But all of that experience *doesn't* replace training any more than all of that hairstylist's experience giving counsel to the women in her salon replaces her need — rather, her *obligation* — to know what she's doing on a professional level before calling herself a coach. And only two things will get her there: training and experience (in that order).

Second, like it or not, as a licensed clinician you are held to a higher standard.

I don't blame you if, at some point while reading the preceding chapters (or maybe right this minute), you're saying to yourself: *I don't need to get trained as a coach, because it's not mandatory. And really, why should I spend my time and money getting trained when some yokel down the street is going straight to market as a self-proclaimed coach? I can out-coach that guy anyway. I'm a therapist, after all.*

Here's my blunt answer to that: You're a trained helping professional, and you're reading this book; the yokel isn't. So though that person can claim ignorance, *you can't*. Just because others are calling themselves "coach" with impunity doesn't mean its fine for you to misrepresent your training and skills. Your ethics and principles cannot be circumstantial. When that happens, they cease to be ethics and principles. And when you lose your ethics and principles, *what on earth are you doing trying to help people in the first place?* Truly, if you've lost your ethics and principles, the person who needs help more than anyone you could possibly reach out to is none other than *you*.

So if that's happening, then I say: *Coach, heal thyself!* Reclaim your sense of professionalism and your integrity, and remember: If you wanted to take the easy road to professional success, you wouldn't have become a therapist in the first place. Sure, money may have been on your mind when you chose this career path, but money isn't enough to get people to the finish line. You really have to be motivated from within and have a strong, inner sense of dedication to not merely become licensed, but then practice day after day. You obviously have all of these things. Now it's time to rekindle that commitment and put it toward coaching.

THE STIGMA OF THERAPY

Another unusual motivating factor that convinces some therapists to label what they do as "coaching"—and in so doing, shortcut the training aspect—comes from the unfortunate reality that there is a stigma associated with the word *therapy*. Indeed, you're probably painfully aware that, truly, clients would prefer *not* to need your services. This isn't personal, and I'm sure you know this. It's simply that the public perception is that folks who need therapy must be screwed up or damaged goods.

Cleverly, some therapists simply avoid this connotation (and all of the implications of it) by changing their label, at least for some clients, from "therapy" to "coaching." In so doing, *superficially* they can focus on all of the positive things that coaching stands for: functional people, goal achievement, and so on.

However, again, as a caution to therapists who are tempted (or who have succumbed to this temptation) to creatively reframe things in this way, I conjure our good ol' friend called *reality*. Because it's reality, and not a label, that will ultimately dictate whether you're a coach (just like reality will reveal to our fictitious hairstylist/coach, sooner rather than later, that she doesn't know what the heck she's doing).

And really, there's a gloriously simple and long-term way to avoid this stigma permanently: get trained as a coach, and practice as a coach. See? Simple. Reality *likes* simple.

LANGUAGE VERSUS REALITY

If the preceding doesn't persuade you about the merits of being trained as a coach, this should clinch it for you: There's *language* (words), and then there's our old friend (yet again) *reality*. Some people think the two are synonymous. Those people are computers. The rest of us, however, use language to *describe* reality, not to define it. And, naturally, we accept that reality defines language. This is what makes language so dynamic—it both describes reality and is in turn shaped by reality.

See the common theme here? If not, let me blurt it out: In the dynamic tandem of reality and language, reality is *predominant*. Reality leads; language follows.

Unfortunately (yes, you knew this was coming, right?), life moves so fast at times that we, individually and culturally, get the two confused. That is, we pay more attention to language and stop paying attention to reality. This is particularly problematic when something *new* emerges onto the scene, something that doesn't have a legacy and history behind it that can keep it on the straight and narrow. For example, if someone out there comes up with a ham sandwich and calls it a laptop computer, let's safely assume that it won't lead to a lot of people walking into Starbucks with a ham sandwich, looking for an outlet and a place to surf the Web. There are simply enough people who know what a laptop is (because laptops have been around for quite a while) for this kind of situation to, well, be absurd (and that's why I picked this example—though if there are any surrealists out there who want to be inspired by this and paint it or something, knock yourselves out!).

My point is, while we know what laptops are (and what ham sandwiches are, for that matter), something like coaching as a helping profession is more problematic because it's *new*. But that newness doesn't mean that we can bury our heads in the proverbial sand and pretend it's not happening; to do that would be to ignore reality. The reality is that there is a helping profession that has emerged called coaching, and as helping professionals we must accept this reality and adjust our language.

And yes, that means folks who are *not* helping professionals—like a drama teacher deciding to call herself a drama coach, or a gardener figuring that the job title "landscaping coach" has a nice ring to it—can, are, and will do what they want to do out of ignorance, carelessness, or sometimes even deliberate deception (i.e., calling oneself a coach exclusively for marketing purposes).

But we as helping professionals must hold ourselves and each other to a higher standard and use language precisely, especially when dealing with the public. And that means, simply, that if you want to be a coach then you need to be trained as one. You need to earn it. The fact that the drama teacher and the gardener aren't doing that cannot be a reason for you to ignore your obligation.

I remember the day I became a therapist in the eyes of the state of California. No, it wasn't the day I achieved my license, which at the time was called "Marriage, Family, and Child Counselor" (MFCC). It was years later, when the state decided to rename it "Marriage and Family Therapist" (MFT). So, whether I liked it or not, my label was "therapist" from that day forth. My work with my clients and my practice didn't change—just the language. Similarly, the word *coach* now describes a helping profession of a certain origin, set of assumptions, and practices. And the public now has a (relatively) *new* choice of helping professionals to choose from. If you call yourself a coach but don't ascribe to the principles and practices of professional coaching, you put yourself on a path of confusing the public and misrepresenting your services. You'll lose out as an individual coach, and by further adding to the confusion around this term, you'll play a role in eroding credibility for us all.

A Word (or Several) on Expertise

While training is valuable (I would say essential) to be an effective — and therefore successful — coach, there is a difference between training and expertise. This difference may, in particular, be confusing to therapists reading this who are wondering to themselves or perhaps muttering aloud: "If I was a client out there and was paying for coaching, I'd want an expert!"

That makes sense, but like many things that make sense, it's not realistic or even necessary (there's a paradox for you!). Remember, clients hire and pay a coach for the coach's ability to help them get the results they want, and *not* for a coach's expertise. Indeed, there are many experts out there on a variety of things, and simply being one of them doesn't mean — at all — that the person has the power to change anything. It simply means that they know a lot of stuff. They have a good memory. All elephants are experts; but would you want to be coached by one? (Actually, that could be very Zen, but that's for another book!)

If the whole expert/nonexpert thing is wearing you down, here's something clear to remember: A coach doesn't need to be an expert in any particular area; coaches simply need to apply their coaching skills expertly. And, unsurprisingly, you learn to do this the old-fashioned way: through training and experience.

Finding the Right Training

Okay: I'm going to comfortably assume that, by this point, you're on board with the view that training is *required* in order for you to be a professional coach. (I can make this assumption because if the preceding discussion hit too close to home and ticked you off, you've stopped reading this book anyway.)

So that means our next focus is on finding the training you need. And that brings us to three options:

Option 1: Start with a *beginner's mind* and enroll in a foundational coach training program.

Option 2: Enroll in a coach training program designed for *therapists*.

Option 3: Enroll in a *specialty* coach training program.

Foundational Coach Training Programs

These comprehensive programs cover all coaching skills from the ground up. If you're like me, you might find yourself a bit (or a lot) impatient with covering basic helping skills that you learned a long time ago as a therapist. However, if you're not like me, you may find it refreshing to simply enter into coaching from the ground floor, and experience it from step one without preconceived notions.

If this option attracts you, I suggest choosing a program that is accredited by the International Coach Federation (ICF) as an Accredited Coach Training Program (ACTP). This ensures that your training will reflect the highest standards and practices of the coaching industry. It will also qualify you for ICF certification, if desired.

In my experience, these are examples of the most established ICF-accredited foundational coach training programs:

- Coach U
- Coaches Training Institute
- New Ventures West
- Newfield Network
- InviteCHANGE (formerly Academy for Coach Training)

Keep in mind that although ICF accreditation increases the likelihood of quality training, if you don't need or desire ICF certification, you're free to get your training anywhere you want.

Coach Training Programs for Therapists

You may want to focus on coach training without going anywhere *near* stuff you already know as a therapist. There are pros and cons to this path. The pros are (surprise) it's faster and more focused, because everything is going to be new or leverage your existing training. The cons are that you may miss out on some perspectives because you're not starting from the ground floor (as you would be with foundational coach training).

If this is the right option for you, here are some programs that specialize in coach training for therapists:

- Institute for Life Coach Training
- MentorCoach
- Hudson Institute
- College of Executive Coaching

Specialty Coach Training Programs

As the name suggests, a specialty coach training program covers a specialized area of coaching. This is a useful way to establish your niche, which is going to be the cornerstone of your marketing (which is discussed later on in this book). However, if you aren't sure which specialty or niche is right for you, then obviously this is not the right option.

If you're interested in pursuing specialty coach training, here are some established, credible organizations that you can consult:

- Relationships: Relationship Coaching Institute (RCI) (full disclosure: I'm the founder of RCI)
- Spirituality: Success Unlimited Network
- Executives: Center for Executive Coaching
- Small and medium-sized businesses: BusinessCoach.com
- Corporations: Corporate Coach U
- Attention deficit disorder/attention deficit/hyperactivity disorder (ADD/ADHD): ADD Coach Academy
- Careers: Career Coach Academy
- Parenting: Parent Coaching Institute

Keep in mind that specialty training programs may not be accredited by the ICF. This is because ICF accreditation applies to coach-specific training programs, which cover core competencies. As such, they don't apply to most of the specialty training programs.

Many More Options Available

The preceding lists are a small sampling of the hundreds of coach training programs available. To learn more:

- Research your options on the ICF website at http://www .coachfederation.org.
- Decide whether in-person or distance learning is best for you.
- Identify a program that fits your professional values, goals, and style.
- Attend an ICF conference and visit the exhibits to review many training programs in one place.
- Interview potential schools and ask to speak to a selection of their graduates.

HOW TO IDENTIFY A GOOD COACH TRAINING PROGRAM

Given the growth of coaching—and that's a *good* thing, overall—you will find many coaching programs beyond those that I've suggested. Here's a list of things to look for when choosing a good (versus a bad) training program:

- **A good training program teaches coaching.**

  This may appear obvious, but just as anyone can call himself or herself a coach, anyone can call a training program "coach training." In fact, many noncoaches are passing along their style of misguided coaching. Look for a clear definition of coaching as distinct from other helping modalities. In other words, if your potential training provider cannot clearly explain to you how their coach training differs from other kinds of training, then that's a red flag and you should look elsewhere.

  Also be sure that your potential training provider is not simply following a fad or using a marketing device by calling their technique "coaching." Investigate to find out if the provider is teaching a model of coaching that applies the skills and principles described in Chapter 2.

- **A good training program provides practicum and mentoring.**

  Training requires doing—not just reading and listening to lectures. Be sure your training program provides you with an adequate opportunity to practice and apply the skills you've learned (most often, you will practice your skills with fellow trainees).

  Additionally, your training program may encourage or facilitate a buddy coach relationship for additional practice. A dyad is great, but a triad is even better, as the observer can provide more input and feedback.

  In addition to experiences with your peers, be sure that your potential training provider gives you the opportunity to observe, be evaluated, and experience coaching with a skilled mentor coach. This might be the instructor, but most often this will be with former graduates who assist with the training. It's important that you work with other *professional* coaches, who can inspire you with examples of how skilled coaches go beyond the mechanics and who can clearly demonstrate and teach the art of coaching.

- **A good training program provides certification.**

  Ensure that your potential training provider prepares you for ICF certification, an internal certification, or both. One reason a provider may not offer ICF certification preparation is simply because it's not applicable. For example, at the Relationship Coaching Institute (RCI), our specialization is relationship coaching, which is not covered by the ICF. We therefore prepare our graduates to earn the internal certifications of Certified Relationship Coach or Master Relationship Coach.

  To be meaningful, the certification that you earn must include supervision and evaluation of your competent work with real clients. A certificate of completion can be compared to sitting through traffic school and passing a written test, and is meaningless for inferring skills acquisition or competence as a coach.

  One question that you might ask is, simply, *Do I need certification?* The answer is . . . maybe!

How to Identify a Good Coach Training Program

As a therapist you already have plenty of credentials and letters after your name, and potential clients generally don't ask you to prove your qualifications unless you don't appear to have any. Therefore, I don't think that certification is essential—unlike training (which *is* essential).

However, obtaining coaching certification can indeed assist you to become a highly skilled and accomplished coach, and demonstrate your commitment to a high standard of professional coaching for your prospective clients. This is helpful in many ways, including marketing.

- **A good training program prepares you to practice.**

It's (unfortunately) common for training providers to focus on skills and strategies for helping your clients in theory, but to leave you clueless as to how it all applies in the real world. Your potential training provider should help you establish things like an intake and assessment process, templates for client forms and contracts, examples of fee structures and service delivery systems, and so on. Though these may seem like the less glamorous aspects of coaching (compared to actually working with people who need help), they are *essential* for operating a successful practice. If your potential training provider isn't supporting you with this learning, you will likely not succeed, even if you're a fabulous coach.

- **A good training program helps you get clients.**

This is my personal favorite insight: You cannot change the world, help a person, or even make a living if you can't get clients. The leaders and staff of your potential training program should have ample experience marketing their services and building a successful practice in the real world, and should pass along their knowledge and strategies to you.

At RCI this is a top priority of ours, and we provide a 12-week comprehensive practice-building program to all participants, as well as models for conducting promotional seminars, classes, and workshops. We list graduates on our website, publish newsletters for the public featuring our graduates, provide referrals from our newsletter subscribers and website visitors, and offer numerous other ways of helping our graduates get clients.

Frankly, though I don't expect many other programs to match RCI in this manner, I would still urge you to choose a training program that pays attention to the practical, real-world business side of being a coach—that is, one that helps you get clients.

Distance Learning Versus In-Person Training

Thanks to Internet technology that is improving on what seems like a monthly basis, there are new training delivery options that flat out didn't exist in the good old days. I drove *a lot* of miles to participate in my first coach training, because as a therapist my only training experience was in person, and I couldn't imagine it any other way.

But things have changed—for the better! These days, most coach training is delivered by distance learning, through the telephone and the Internet. If you're wondering about the effectiveness of distance learning, I can only tell you that in my (slightly biased) opinion, it's possible to do *everything* over the telephone and the Internet that you can do in person, much more conveniently and at a much lower cost than in-person training (as long as the training is live with human instructors and not 100% online).

Some coach training programs conduct their trainings only in person (such as Coaches Training Institute, New Ventures West, Hudson Institute, and Newfield Network). Others offer only distance learning (such as Relationship Coaching Institute, Coach U, Institute for Life Coach Training, and MentorCoach); and some use a combination (such as inviteCHANGE).

Which approach is right for you? There are many variables for you to consider, such as course availability, cost, convenience, time away from your family or practice, and so on. All things being equal (which, of course, they're not, but it's fun to say these kinds of things), I would simply suggest that you choose the training approach that excites you and resonates with who you are and how you want to practice as a coach.

CAN I BE A COACH AND A THERAPIST?

In a word: yes!

There is nothing preventing you, structurally, morally, ethically, or any other way, from being both a coach and a therapist (or a therapist and a coach, if you prefer). In fact, in doing so you'll likely discover that it enables your practice to serve more people in better ways. Coaching gives you a powerful service modality to offer prospective clients, when it's appropriate and in their best interest to do so.

To keep matters simple, I suggest that you develop parallel, yet distinct practices: one for your work as a therapist, the other for your work as a coach. And by "distinct" I *mean* distinct: you should have separate business cards, websites, fee structures, client agreement forms, advertising and marketing campaigns, and so on.

Think of your coaching practice as an entirely different business from your therapy practice. Start with a blank slate, and ask yourself: *Who do I want to coach? What kind of coaching do I want to do? What will be my specialty and niche? How do I want to deliver my coaching services?*

A great way to keep your therapy and coaching practices separate is to have different specialties and niches. For example, if you specialize in couples therapy, marketing yourself as a relationship coach for couples risks confusion and overlap. Focusing on relationship coaching for singles would be a good complement in this situation.

As you go through these questions, don't let fear of the unknown keep you from moving forward. Instead, see this scenario for what it is: a wonderful opportunity! You can take *everything* you know, all that you are, and reinvent yourself as a helping professional. Life doesn't (seem to) offer these kinds of invitations to change all that regularly, so make sure you take advantage of this one.

My own experience has been that, once I embraced coaching and allowed it to peacefully coexist alongside my work as a therapist, I was energized by an unleashing of creativity and entrepreneurial spirit. It was so powerful, in fact, that it led to the creation of my book *Conscious Dating: Finding the Love of Your Life in Today's World*. I never imagined writing a book as a therapist, let alone pioneering a whole coaching program for singles. You, too, might find that coaching allows you to help people in ways that you never imagined, and inspires you to create specialized products and services that make a real contribution to the world.

CAN YOU PROVIDE THERAPY *AND* COACHING TO THE SAME CLIENT AT THE SAME TIME?

Generally speaking: no. It's my strong opinion that you can't and shouldn't provide coaching and therapy to the *same* client at the *same* time. Both approaches, while complementing each other in many ways, are still different. Furthermore, your relationship with your client is different, too. Here are the reasons why:

o As a therapist, you're positioned as the expert. This is not only the role you assume, but it's frankly the one that your client wants you to assume, too. This creates a basic, fundamental asymmetrical power relationship that never changes. Though this works (sometimes) in therapy, it's incompatible with coaching, where the client is the expert, and the coach is more of a skilled, trained, and compassionate facilitator/enabler.

o As a therapist, you're typically dealing with your clients' most vulnerable emotional areas and issues, which can lead to a transference-countertransference relationship. Because of this, when you ask a client to stretch beyond that, you can risk undermining the integrity (and the safety, security, and appropriateness) of the relationship. Coaching, in contrast, not only bypasses this limitation, but it outright *invites* bypassing it; in fact, coaching is all about stretching beyond barriers. In coaching, you *want* to get to a place where you can reasonably and responsibly hold clients accountable for their actions and, ultimately, their outcomes and results.

o On the heels of the preceding point, I don't believe that, once established, the transference-countertransference relationship ends when a client graduates—it just lingers. Coaching, by design, alertly prevents the transference-countertransference relationship from taking root at all. This is good news in the short term (i.e., working with a client to achieve a goal), and even better news in the long term, because the same client may (and probably will) want to work with you in the future to achieve *another* goal. Because transference-countertransference isn't lingering and ready to manifest and weaken or even harm the relationship, it's a much cleaner, simpler path to achieving the next goal.

o As a therapist, you address problems, issues, dysfunction, and causality. In coaching, you address solutions and barriers to progressive, positive growth. You don't spend time and effort on the negative; it's there, and analyzing it (and analyzing it . . . and analyzing it) to its roots is meaningless and even harmful, because it wastes valuable time. The focus is on solutions and growth. It's on getting from A to B, not on *why* someone is stuck on A.

o As a therapist, you most likely diagnose, develop a treatment plan, bill insurance, provide a receipt for medical reimbursement and deductions, and so on. Coaching takes a different and simpler path: direct billing. (As an aside: It's been my experience, surprisingly, that some clients who pay directly for coaching actually make *more* progress, because there is some incentive to keep things practical and realistic—not theoretical and abstract.)

However, it's certainly possible—and in some cases, quite beneficial—for you to provide therapy and coaching to the same client; just not at the same time. For example, you can create a program whereby, once clients graduate from therapy with you, they join your coaching group for ongoing support, to apply what they've learned and to continue their growth and development. I'll discuss this further in Chapter 4.

With all of that having been said, it *may* be possible to coach your therapy client if:

- Your style of therapy is more strategic, cognitive-behavioral, brief, problem-solving, action-oriented; a style more compatible

with coaching that minimizes the risk of developing an emotionally bonded transference-countertransference relationship.
- Your client is emotionally healthy and resilient, takes responsibility, and is functional in all aspects of life.
- Your client responds to your coaching and experiences success
(do not continue unsuccessful coaching!).

Remember: Coaching a therapy client has the potential to backfire
and result in a malpractice suit. You must be *very* confident that your
client is ready and functional enough for this relationship with you,
and your motivation needs to truly be in the service of the client's
best interests.

Also keep in mind that, while you can move from therapy to coaching with a client—carefully, gently, and appropriately—there are
some hazards to watch out for, including:

- The client's dysfunction is rarely cured—growth and healing
are a process that takes years, and when you treat dysfunction, you can't assume that it's gone because the client appears
better.
- Even a client-centered therapy approach includes treatment
and an asymmetrical relationship that you can't reverse. You
will *always* be that client's therapist and responsible for addressing the therapeutic needs that brought the client to you. If you
believe in the transference-countertransference dynamic of therapy (which is less in some modalities), this doesn't disappear
when your client progresses and you transition to coaching.

In my own situation, my style of therapy and my style of coaching
are so different that I can't imagine combining them with the same
client. Further, it's not an issue for me, since I long ago arrived at
the point in my practice where I preferred coaching (and referred
therapy clients to my colleagues).

Also be aware that if you determine that a coaching client would
benefit from therapy, then you still might also be able to provide
coaching. For example, a client may come to see you as a therapist

for multiple symptoms, and you may believe that coaching—not therapy—would work faster than catering to those symptoms. In this situation, I would say that, generally, clients who want to address their symptoms are really therapy clients, not coaching clients. This is because they generally have an idea of what they want, or a pre-conceived notion of what to expect, and this needs to be addressed through therapy. However, if you assess that they could indeed benefit from coaching, then simply discuss your recommendation and reasoning with them. You might choose to explain it this way: The symptoms are the what, and the approach to them is the how. Then let them choose which is more important: the what or the how. You may be surprised how many folks really want the how explained more than the what, since they're more focused on the results they want.

Or you might find yourself with a client who wants coaching and resists therapy (by the way, most of these clients are disproportionately male!). Either way, if you believe that therapy alongside coaching would be a value to your client, then put it in your contract that you'll provide coaching only if the client also sees a therapist. Then make following through and working effectively with the therapist part of the coaching agenda (by the way, therapists really appreciate this!).

WATCH OUT, DOC

An interesting problem that can emerge as you transition from therapist to coach revolves around power and persona. As a therapist, you're familiar with your role as the expert in the relationship with your client. However, this role is incompatible with the equal partnership of coaching, which emphasizes that the client is the expert of herself or himself—even if you are the one who knows the modality, the concepts, the terms, and so on. In other words, you must engage your client as a peer, not as a subordinate.

This can be an added challenge if everything in your office suggests that you're an expert (e.g., title, degrees, certifications on the wall, a giant flashing neon sign that blinks I AM AN EXPERT AND YOU ARE NOT, etc.). You also don't want to be called *Doctor* by your coaching clients. You want them to call you by your first name, just like any other peer.

Be aware that assuming the expert role can happen even if you don't consciously, overtly take on that role. The client may put you in that role. For example, I've had clients insist on calling me "Dr. Steele" even after I've informed them that I don't have a PhD, and I prefer to simply be called "David." Watch yourself, and guard against slipping into the expert role—*especially* when your client wants you to.

If this becomes an obstacle, consider providing your coaching services in a different location (or over the phone). You might also benefit from other visual cues and reminders, such as an affirmation that you keep on your desk or anything else that helps you know that when you're coaching, you aren't the expert. Don't feel bad if it takes a while to get used to this. At first, it's disorienting because it's not what you're accustomed to. However, if you embrace your new reality, chances are it will reward you with the courage and energy you need to easily transition from therapist to coach. In fact, you may (like me) find that coaching expands to become your *only* modality.

COACHING HAS A WAY OF EXPANDING

When I began my coaching career, my intention was to practice both therapy and coaching. However, I found coaching to be so much more fun, more effective, and indeed more profitable (which is always nice) that I allowed my therapy practice to dwindle, built a full coaching practice within three months, and within six months no longer had any therapy clients while coaching represented 100% of my practice. This wasn't by design. It's simply how things unfolded.

Your experience may not be similar to mine, but don't be shocked if it is. There is something very attractive about coaching that starts to make more sense the more you practice it, and the more people who are helped *through* it. Or you may find yourself doing something that I'll dub "thera-coaching," which is therapy that includes coaching strategies and skills, but isn't formally coaching because the service bills insurance, provides treatment for a disorder, establishes an asymmetrical relationship between client and therapist-coach, and so on.

My point is that even if you don't become a full-blown, flag-waving coach like me, just bringing coaching into your world as a therapist — to any extent — is a positive, helpful outcome that should be celebrated because it will help both you and the people you aim to help.

CHAPTER FOUR

Integrating Coaching into Your Therapy Practice

How will you set your fees?

Do you need different liability insurance?

What are the legal implications?

Can you bill medical insurance for coaching?

Do you need different forms for coaching?

How are coaching sessions different from therapy sessions?

Do you market your coaching services differently?

This chapter dives into some of the more pragmatic aspects of coaching—setting fees, creating forms, and the all-important question of whether you should provide coaching or therapy services to a client.

Let me emphasize the "or" near the end of the preceding sentence. As you learned in the first three chapters, it's neither necessary nor even arguably beneficial for you to replace your therapy practice with a coaching practice. True, this may happen over time if it's rewarding for you to do so, but there's no need to choose one or the other. The purpose of this book, as I hope you agree by now, is to help you transition coaching into your practice. The velocity at which you do this, and the rewards that result, will determine whether coaching *becomes* your practice, as was the case with me.

Also take comfort from knowing that everything we discuss in this chapter applies even if you transition to 100% coaching—especially if you plan to maintain your clinical license. Frankly, your licensing board is not overly concerned with what you call your service ("coaching," "therapy," "neuro-linguistic programming (NLP)," "emotional freedom techniques (EFT)," and so on). To the licensing board, *everything* you do falls under your license.

SETTING FEES: THERAPY

As you know, therapy sessions are typically billed by the hour *after* the service has been rendered. And these hourly rates are often set by seeing what other therapists of comparable experience in the same area are charging.

What really happens, regardless of a stated hourly fee, is that most therapists accept a discounted rate for insurance reimbursement. Plus, they often offer a "sliding scale" or negotiate their fees when uninsured clients balk at what seems like an overly expensive hourly rate, regardless of ability to pay. Although the short-term results of this are rewarding—therapists can help clients who otherwise would find the fee prohibitive—the long-term results, from a business perspective, are punitive. Through no fault of their own, the same clients who enjoyed a discounted fee naturally tell friends and family about this "great therapist with amazingly low rates." Before long, more and more clients pay discounted rates and, taken as a whole, can create financial instability for a practice (if not outright financial havoc).

What exacerbates this billing dynamic in therapy is the fact that, in my experience, therapists in general seem to have a . . . *dysfunctional* relationship with money and, in particular, *making* money or that evil, horrible p-word: profit. It's as if there is something inherently unethical about charging clients a fair market price for a valuable service. Really, this is an issue born out of lack of self-worth, and it often manifests as an inability to say no to a client who can't or won't pay a stated hourly rate. The result, again, is discounting rates to the point where a therapist is simply not earning fair market value.

Now, the purpose of this book isn't to address this dysfunction, but if you find yourself affected by what I've written—perhaps even a touch offended—then let me speak directly to you: Accepting discounted fees, whether insurance reimbursement or private pay, *is a disservice to yourself and your client.* If you earn less than you feel you deserve, then you will consciously or unconsciously resent your client for playing a role in that equation, however unintentional or blameless. That resentment interferes with your ability to help. So in a (brutally) honest way, when you discount your fees, you're also *discounting your service.* It's an equilibrium.

However, there are times where limited pro bono services work from both an ethical and a professional point of view. More on this topic in Chapter 7.

SETTING FEES: COACHING

Ideally, most therapists would prefer a client to commit to weekly sessions over a period of months and not have each session become a "buy or not buy" decision. Coaching accomplishes this easily and naturally.

Coaching is typically billed *in advance* by the month. This is because, as we all know—therapists, coaches, and anyone else formally or even informally aware of the helping process—real change occurs over time; it's not a light switch that flicks on. It's more of a dimmer switch, gradually getting brighter with each session.

Because of this, most coaches require new clients to commit to one to three months. In fact, I've seen coaches who require a full-year commitment or more! And although this might seem long in terms of both time and finances, you might be surprised at how many clients are open to this.

The idea of making a commitment to on-going coaching is a paradigm shift for therapists. Yes, it's what they'd *like* to do, but it's not what they *can* do, given the limited billing options. But this par-adigm shift (or *shock* might be the more apt term) makes a lot of good, old-fashioned common sense when you realize that coaches should *never* view their service as exchanging their time for money. They aren't getting paid by the hour. They're getting paid by the month, because they're helping clients get results and achieve their most important goals. Looking at professional life in terms of an hour is extremely limiting and unnecessary. It's also fruitless, since no client is going to change from 2 P.M. to 3 P.M., regardless of how great a coach you are or will be. The more appropriate time frame is a month, a quarter, half a year, or even a year, depending on the goals that need to be achieved.

WHAT KIND OF CLIENTS DO YOU WANT?

This is an odd question for therapists, especially those who rely on word-of-mouth marketing (i.e., passive marketing). As long as clients aren't a danger to themselves or others, the kind of client a therapist wants is one that the calendar says is coming in that day.

Coaching is more deliberate; it is more active and therefore requires more awareness (and some might say more responsibility, too). The kinds of clients you see as a coach should be integrated into your business plan and the niche that you'll service. I'll focus more on choosing a niche and finding ideal clients later on in this book, but for now it's enough to share with you that the kinds of clients you want as a coach include those who are

- motivated,
- supportable and able to benefit from your coaching, and
- willing and able to pay your fees.

Naturally, then, you'll design your coaching practice to embrace these kinds of clients. Plus, you'll confidently set your fees high enough and position yourself to attract clients who will pay your full rate. Note that I didn't say "afford your full rate." That implies, subtly, that you're making a demand on your prospective clients that they are unnaturally expected to meet (i.e., they wouldn't otherwise do it on their own). But this is not about that at all, so the word *afford* has no place here. You simply set an appropriate fee and attract clients who find it to be a fair, reasonable rate for your coaching services.

That said, I do appreciate—and have personal experience with—the challenge that, as a coach, you'll need to be more selective with your clientele than you were or are as a therapist. This can unleash all kinds of latent feelings about self-worth or even whether there is something patently unethical about being selective at all. These are barriers that you, as a coach, will need to courageously face and, in doing so, determine what is a valid insight and what is destructive toxic self-talk.

My low-risk prediction is that you'll find much of the discomfort is not related to what's going on out there in the world at all, but rather, it is based in your own opinion of yourself as a helping professional. When you tackle this dragon and slay it under the gaze of your conscious awareness, you'll find that being selective about clients is not immoral. Nor is it honorable. It's simply a neutral fact that influences how you run your practice—nothing more, nothing less.

LIABILITY INSURANCE: YES OR NO?

It's my goal to provide you with as much clarity as possible in this book and to avoid ambivalent answers. However, life is full of ambivalence (there's a paradox in there somewhere). So I must admit that the answer to whether you need liability insurance is a rather unsatisfying but honest: maybe yes, maybe no.

Start with this: Do you have liability insurance now? If so, it's most likely because your insurance company and other third-party reimbursement sources require it. And it makes sense. As a therapist, you deal with people's deepest vulnerabilities. Accusations of malpractice are a risk that you and third-party reimbursers want protection from.

Now, your licensing board doesn't care what you call your service—Eye Movement Desensitization and Reprocessing (EMDR), Emotionally Focused Therapy (EFT), brief therapy, hypnosis, coaching, counseling, consultation, and so on. *Everything* that you do with clients falls under your license. Likewise, your liability insurance covers your work with your clients, regardless of the treatment modality.

However, there are two exceptions:

1. Your policy has specific exclusions (read the fine print).
2. Your policy doesn't cover telephone sessions, workshops, and other services conducted outside your office, and other activities that you might conduct as a coach different from a traditional therapy practice (again, read the fine print, and contact your insurer if you're unclear).

If, as a therapist, you need additional liability insurance for your coaching practice because your current liability insurance doesn't cover certain coaching activities and services, I recommend getting liability insurance *specifically* for coaches, which is readily available and inexpensive.

Also keep in mind that many coaches (who either, like me, aren't practicing therapy of any kind or, mostly, were never therapists to begin with) don't carry liability insurance. They don't do this simply to save the premium. They do it because carrying insurance is in itself a noncoaching statement that, ironically, could invite litigation. It could convey a message that coaching is a kind of therapy that has risks and requires liability insurance.

OTHER LEGAL CONSIDERATIONS

I'm not a lawyer, a legal expert, or even that annoying guy at a dinner party who *pretends* to be a lawyer or legal expert. However, I do know some legal experts, and it's through them that I've gleaned some general information that, to my knowledge, is true. (However, let me also add that since laws and regulations can change, and they vary from state to state and jurisdiction to jurisdiction, please always consult with a qualified legal expert to make sure that what may be true in another area of the country is also true where you live and practice.)

As we've discussed in earlier chapters, unlike licensed helping professions that are highly regulated, coaching is currently a self-regulated and unlicensed profession. However, this doesn't mean that it's the

Wild West and anyone can and should do anything they wish. Just because a profession isn't licensed doesn't mean that it can function outside the laws, regulations, and standards of society.

To ensure that you establish yourself on the right side of any issues both legally and ethically, I strongly recommend you assume that all requirements of your therapist's license apply to your coaching services. Remember: Your licensing board and the courts probably won't care that you call your service "coaching" if you are in violation of a law or regulation that applies to your license. (And yes, this means that you *will* be held to a higher standard than coaches without a clinical license.)

The following are some other general legal issues and concepts that you'll want to be clear about as you establish and grow your coaching practice:

- **Malpractice.** The primary consideration for legal and ethical practices is clearly this: What is in the best interest of the client? That means that even if an action doesn't break the law, if it's allegedly harmful to a client, a coach can be held civilly liable.
- **Fraud or misrepresentation.** It's illegal to say or publish statements that are untrue or unproven. Unfortunately, this is a gray area that many coaches cross when they use hyped-up marketing language that promises results that cannot be delivered.
- **Privacy.** Most licensed professionals are familiar with the privacy requirements of the Health Insurance Portability and Accountability Act (HIPAA). Arguably, the obligation to keep and store records, maintain client confidentiality (more on this in the next point), and so on are not, for a coach, legal concerns so much as they are ethical concerns. This is because, according to some, harm (such as defamation) has to be proven before an issue becomes legal. However, as previously stated, I strongly recommend that you assume that all requirements of your license apply to your coaching services.
- **Confidentiality.** Coaching, like therapy, is a confidential relationship. Clients must feel free to share information with you and trust that you will not misuse that information or reveal it

in ways that could cause harm. There is a clear ethical requirement, though not a legal requirement, for coaches to maintain confidentiality. This means that if a lawsuit can prove harm, you could be held civilly liable.

- **Privilege.** Unlike doctor-patient and therapist-client relationships, the coach-client relationship is *not* legally privileged and you *can* be compelled to testify in court to reveal confidential information. You could attempt to invoke privilege by using your status as a licensed professional, but be aware that if it is established that your service was coaching and not therapy, this won't work.

- **Mail and e-mail solicitations.** Collecting and using client contact information to send marketing-oriented material is regulated by the Federal Trade Commission. Ensure that you publish a privacy policy, get permission to add contact information to a mailing list, and comply with mailing list removal requests.

- **Dual relationships.** Although certain kinds of dual or multiple-role relationships are often limited or prohibited in mental health licensing ethics codes and professional codes of ethics, most are not prevented in coaching. In fact, coaching has its origins in settings such as the business world where dual relationships are common. Although you might relax your boundaries with coaching clients and socialize or barter services with them, conflicts of interest and sexual relationships with coaching clients are unethical—and harm can easily be proven. Although losing a lawsuit typically won't remove your ability to practice as a coach, you could lose your license, reputation, and assets.

- **Abuse reporting and duty to warn.** Unlike therapists, coaches are not typically mandated to report abuse or to warn threatened parties. However, if harm can be proven by your actions or inaction, you could lose a civil lawsuit. Again—and I know I keep saying this, but there's a reason for my repetition—my strong recommendation for the therapist-coach is to assume that all requirements of your clinical license will apply to your coaching services as well.

PROTECTING YOURSELF FROM VIOLATIONS

To protect yourself from accusations of legal or ethical violations, I recommend that you

- obtain professional liability insurance for your coaching services, and
- use a written coaching contract/agreement that clearly spells out the nature of the coaching relationship, expectations of client and coach, and ethical practices, such as confidentiality and privacy.

Additionally, when you're unsure of what to do in any given client-related situation, I recommend that you do these three things:

1. Review the International Coach Federation (ICF) Code of Ethics and your licensing regulations.
2. Ask an experienced mentor coach for advice.
3. Ask yourself: "Would I be proud of my actions if this situation came to light in the media or in court?"

CAN YOU BILL MEDICAL INSURANCE FOR COACHING?

After the murkiness of the preceding sections it's refreshing to sink into something so utterly definitive: You *cannot* bill medical insurance for coaching, and you shouldn't even think about it. Here are three reasons why:

1. Insurance billing pays for "medically necessary" services, whereas coaching is *not* medically necessary. I repeat: Coaching is *not* medically necessary.
2. Insurance billing typically requires a diagnosis and treatment plan, whereas coaching does not use a diagnosis and treatment plan model.
3. Insurance billing means the client will not pay the full fee out of pocket. This lessens a client's financial investment in the outcome, which is a practice and attitude that is not compatible with coaching.

And what happens if you find prospective coaching clients who will work with you only if you bill their insurance? If you can't educate them on the difference between therapy and coaching, and emphasize that insurance will *not* pay for coaching (and shouldn't), then politely show them the door or hang up the phone. You don't want this kind of client. They aren't open to the very concept of coaching, and that openness is vital to their success in coaching. Be thankful that you're finding out very early that they are not candidates for coaching.

DO YOU NEED DIFFERENT FORMS FOR COACHING?

In a word: yes.

In more words: you should have a coaching client contract that includes many of the same disclosures as your therapy forms, including confidentiality (and exceptions), abuse reporting, and so on. This contract should also detail the minimum commitment required, fees and payment procedures, refund policy (if any), and so on.

In general, good coaching agreements

- spell out the nature of the coaching relationship;
- describe the expectations for the client;
- describe the expectations for the coach;
- state the definition and focus of coaching versus therapy;
- specify the exceptions to confidentiality (if any);
- specify that although the coach is a therapist, the coach won't be providing therapy; and
- explain that coaching is not a substitute for therapy, and that if the client seeks therapy from another professional, the client must notify the therapist of the coaching.

Templates for these agreements are available from most coach training programs, some books on coaching, and the ICF website.

In your intake process, be sure to explicitly and clearly address your new client's understanding and expectations of coaching. Most problems and lawsuits occur because expectations are violated.

THE STRUCTURE AND DURATION OF COACHING SESSIONS

As a coach, you have a variety of options for session structure and duration (unlike most therapy sessions, where the 50-minute hour reigns supreme).

In terms of duration, there is no defined length, either formally or generally. Some coaches schedule one-hour sessions, while others cap it at 10 minutes. When deciding how long to meet with your coaching clients, ask yourself what would be the most effective length. Then ask yourself if you're willing to commit to that length. Find the (same) number that satisfies both questions.

Now, these two questions may seem weird, especially the second one. However, sometimes you must honestly admit that even though your new client would benefit from, say, 90-minute sessions, you may not have the availability (or the desire) to meet for 90 minutes without throwing off your whole schedule.

By asking both questions, you prevent yourself from unintentionally mulling over *only* duration possibilities that already fit your preconceived tolerances. In simpler terms: If you will provide *only* 15-minute or 30-minute coaching sessions (for whatever reason), then there is a temptation to ask yourself: "Should I provide 15-minute or 30-minute sessions for this new client? Which of the two is better for them?"

As you can see, this is a flawed question; it's disingenuous. You're already limiting things because of your duration preference. You're trying to fit your client into your (duration) box, rather than honestly determining what's best for him or her. Sometimes, you'll simply not be able to provide the right kind of coaching because of duration.

If that happens, you may have to simply not provide coaching to those clients. Or you may have to have an honest, direct conversation with them, explaining your thought process, and giving the clients the opportunity to decide what's best for them. If they decide to find another coach, then you have to respect their decision to do that.

In terms of structure, I know coaches who help their clients experience amazing results by working intensively one-on-one for days or weeks at a time, then gradually moving into a monthly "check and maintain" approach. I've also known of other coaches who check in with their clients for a few minutes daily or weekly, and supplement that communication with e-mail correspondence.

Ultimately, the structure will reflect the unique dynamics of you as a coach (i.e., what you can do) and the needs of your client. If there's a guiding principle to help you succeed here, it's simply to remain flexible and be willing to tailor your services to your client's needs. This is a departure (to say the least!) from therapy, where the structure is very solid and predictable and predetermined by the therapist.

MARKETING YOUR COACHING SERVICES

Later in this book, we focus on how to market and cover key aspects such as choosing a niche, branding your practice, and other elements that will help you succeed.

However, because in this chapter we're addressing distinctions between what you're used to as a therapist and what you can expect as a coach, it's a good idea to understand the key considerations and differences between marketing your therapy services and marketing your coaching services as a therapist/coach.

- **Target audience.** As a coach, you'll be marketing your services toward functional people who are actively looking to make improvements. By "actively looking" I mean that these people are *emotionally motivated* to find a solution to their challenges and don't have to be talked into or convinced of this fact. You can easily get their attention by marketing solutions that address their needs and goals.

  Your marketing in its myriad of forms—website, online marketing, print marketing, speaking engagements, and so on—will target *functional* and *solution-oriented* clients. Compare this with your marketing as a therapist (if it exists at all), which is no doubt geared toward *dysfunctional* and probably *passive* clients with serious problems who would rather not need your services.

- **Referral sources.** As a coach, your clients will be referred to you from a wide variety of sources—well beyond what you're used to as a therapist (medical professionals, other professional service providers, insurance companies, etc.). For example, as a coach it's not uncommon to receive referrals after giving a speaking engagement to a group of any kind—everyone from salespeople to lawyers to entrepreneurs to, in my experience, single people looking for stronger, healthier relationships.

- **Testimonials.** As a coach, you'll both invite and (with permission, of course) publish testimonials from your clients, which will serve as powerful marketing tools that can ethically influence future prospective clients. For therapists, however, this kind of marketing must be approached very carefully. Client confidentiality must be protected, and most practitioners frown upon testimonials—even with client permission. Furthermore, most therapy clients, understandably, don't want to broadcast their involvement in therapy in the first place!

- **Referral fees.** Commissions are frowned upon for obtaining therapy clients but are common for some forms of marketing coaching (workshops, seminars, classes, products, etc.) that utilize online transactions that can be tracked to the referral source (known as affiliate commissions).

- **Advertising.** As a coach, advertising can help you reach your target markets. However, as a therapist you probably already have some form of advertising in place, even if it's just yellow pages advertising, or possibly a website. Therefore, advertising probably doesn't need to be introduced into your world as much as it needs to be *expanded*. There are simply more opportunities to appropriately advertise coaching than there are to advertise therapy. Why? Again (sorry for being repetitious, but this is a point you never want to forget), coaching is about targeting functional, healthy people who want to be *more functional* and *healthier*. It's not about targeting *dysfunctional* people who want to avoid becoming *less healthy*. Consequently, there are simply more advertising opportunities that are appropriate for coaching. It's a positive, progressive message.

- **Specialty and niche.** Marketing, very simply, is communicating what you do. To be effective, your marketing must target a particular audience or niche. As a coach, I advise you (and will further advise you later in this book) to create a coaching specialty, and then offer it to a targeted niche. This is because it's simply a more effective and efficient way of structuring your marketing and branding your practice to reach your desired prospective clients. Many therapists, whether they are generalists or specialists, typically work with all kinds of clients. Thus, any marketing that therapists do is typically not targeted at all, in terms of either its message or its audience.

- **Websites and Internet marketing.** This is a *huge* topic that we'll explore later in this book. For now, however, it's enough to note that as a coach, you'll certainly want to immerse yourself (or at least have someone immerse your practice) into aspects of Internet marketing that fit your business strategy for your niche. This includes creating a functional, sophisticated website—and not just a brochure on the Web. Plus, this means using Internet systems and tools such as social media and mobile media to brand your practice, target your niche, develop your prospects, and maintain or grow your client base. This is a rather dramatic departure from what most therapists do on the Internet, which—if anything—is usually limited to a simple, nonfunctional website describing their services and bio, and the use of e-mail. This is discussed more in Chapter 7.

A NOTE ABOUT CLIENT ENROLLMENT

Prospective therapy clients typically self-identify that they need therapy and make the first contact. Enrolling clients as a therapist is typically a straightforward process: They're referred to you by someone they trust or their insurance company, and enrollment is really a matter of paperwork and scheduling. Even private-pay therapy client enrollment is relatively easy. Once the prospective client becomes convinced that a therapist or therapy can help them, they usually move forward, not wishing to delay addressing their distress.

Enrolling clients as a coach, however, is often a different story. Prospective coaching clients are usually created through referrals and your marketing efforts. There are few, if any, prospective coaching clients who self-identify that they want coaching and seek out a coach. Most enrollment conversations are initiated by the coach. Prospective coaching clients are typically more skeptical, have more questions and reservations, and need to come to know, like, and trust coaches in order to make the leap and hire them. There is more of a relationship-building dialogue between the initial meeting (whether that's on the phone, in person, or even through e-mail) and the commencement of coaching services. Successfully ushering a client through the enrollment process is a key skill that all coaches must master to have a successful practice. Note, however, that this has nothing to do with *selling*. It's simply a respectful conversation where both the prospective client and the coach explore whether there is a beneficial fit (remember, the fit has to be from the *coach's* side, too, not just from the client's side). This is discussed further in Chapter 8.

A FINAL WARNING

Before moving on, here are some warnings about marketing and getting clients that you'll want to remember throughout your coaching career.

First, coaches and therapists will commonly offer to meet with prospective clients at no charge to determine compatibility and help the prospective client make an informed hiring decision. That makes sense. However, what *doesn't* make sense—at least not financial sense—is when both therapists and coaches turn this into a no-charge consultation and even brand it as such (sometimes calling it a "free initial consultation," "sample session," or something similar). The difference here is that they are communicating that they are providing a free service rather than conducting a getting-to-know-you meeting to determine compatibility. My advice here is simple: Don't do this. Free consultations typically invite lookie loos who are just window-shopping and people who want free advice. Free initial consultations are, at best, marginally effective for getting private-pay clients and counterproductive in the long term when you consider the real value of your limited time. By all means, continue offering no-charge meetings to confirm suitability and compatibility; just don't allow them to devolve into mini sessions where you give away your valuable services. This is discussed more in Chapter 8.

Second, I've seen that new coaches will sometimes offer clients a choice of how often to meet per month. They'll charge a lower fee for fewer meetings per month, and a higher fee for more frequent meetings per month. This is a mistake! However well-intentioned, this structure puts a dollar value on the coaching session instead of where the emphasis both logically and ethically needs to be: on the results. This structure also encourages (if not outright convinces) clients to choose their level of coaching based on cost instead of effectiveness. To avoid this, I recommend that you

- design a coaching alliance that's effective for the client,
- set a flat fee per month for all of your coaching clients, and
- *do not* discount your monthly fee for fewer sessions.

Again, I dive further into marketing and enrolling clients later in this book. It's now time to transition from the practice of coaching to building a coaching business.

CHAPTER FIVE

Choosing Your Coaching Niche

What is a niche?

The benefits of choosing a niche.

How do you choose a niche?

How to own your niche.

Can you coach more than one niche?

In this chapter I focus on a topic so important to having a successful coaching practice that it could be a book unto itself.

Indeed, understanding what a niche *is*, what a niche *isn't*, and how to make a niche work for you is arguably the most important marketing element for you to learn in this book. So please, do yourself and your practice a big favor and carefully read, reread, and refer back to this chapter as you build and grow your practice. With some experience under your belt, you'll clearly see the wisdom in doing this (and then you'll be saying this to other coaches who look at you strangely when you plead for them to learn about niches).

So, allow me to begin this chapter by making three strong declarations:

1. All effective marketing is niche marketing (it targets a particular audience).

2. Effective marketing requires communicating to and for your desired audience, not yourself.
3. Unless you target a niche, you can market till the cows come home and you won't get any clients.

What Is a Niche?

Here's the simplest (and by no coincidence, the most accurate) way to understand a niche: Your niche answers the fundamentally important question of *whom do you help?*

Now, at first glance (and maybe second, third, and tenth glance) this seems like a weird question. Obviously, you know who you are as a professional, right? Or . . . maybe not? Pause for a moment and really stare into this question. Do you really know whom you help? Or, like so many people, are you much better informed and clearer about *what you do?*

Ah, therein lies the source of the great confusion that surrounds the whole concept of niches. Most people focus on what they do—but that is *not* a niche; it's a specialization. And while choosing a specialization is essential these days (more on this later), focusing on only this aspect of your coaching will not help you with your marketing, at least not in an effective way. That's because you'll be focusing (like many specialists erroneously do) on your credentials, skills, abilities, and so on—instead of the people whom those credentials, skills, and abilities are aimed toward.

I'm a pragmatist, and if coaches (among other helping professionals) were calling something a niche when it was really a specialization, or calling something a specialization when it was really a niche, or calling it *anything* or *nothing* and it was nevertheless working for them, I would not waste anyone's time (including my own) by highlighting it with such intensity in this chapter. But my motivation goes far, far deeper than the cosmetics or aesthetics of proper marketing terminology.

The problem is that if you focus on your specialization (what you do), your marketing message will be misguided and weak; and any business you derive from it will likely be *in spite of* your marketing rather than because of it. This is because you'll be focusing on yourself: what services you provide, why you're qualified, and so on. These aspects are important, but they don't — at all — reach out to your ideal client and say: *Hello there, I can help you!* And when your marketing fails to do that — directly or indirectly, as appropriate — then, frankly, your marketing fails. Yes, some generous and open-minded prospective clients will often do your marketing for you; that is, they will connect the dots between how great you are as a coach and how you can help them. But many prospective clients won't. They're not going to do your work for you. They'll simply respond to some other coach who reaches out into their world and says *I'm here to help*.

That leads to another insight that I've implied, but need to make explicit: When you choose a niche, you accept that *you cannot be all things to all people*. This is a huge obstacle for many generalists who don't want to limit their possible client base. Unfortunately, whether they choose to realize it or not, my clear experience is that generalization *in itself* is already limiting the possible client base. In other words, people out there who might otherwise become clients are not doing so because the generalist's marketing message doesn't appeal to them; it doesn't *reach* them.

Furthermore — and this is where we get to the heart of things (thank you for your patience) — when you choose a niche, you vastly increase both the content potential and the channel potential of your marketing. Let me explain both those terms for you.

- **Content potential.** When you identify your niche, you start to discover the kinds of messages that you can create to target the prospective clients in that niche. Take me, for example. My profession is that I'm a coach. My *specialization* is that I'm a relationship coach. But my *niche* might be Silicon Valley singles who want to consciously find their soul mate. By knowing my niche, I'm able to create all kinds of focused content that appeals to this group. Whether it's my website, my brochures, or any other kind of marketing that I wish to do, I know — because my niche tells me — to whom I'm speaking.
- **Channel potential.** When you start crafting marketing messages for your niche, you can also effectively choose the ways — or

channels—of reaching them. Again, I'll use an example from my life to make this easy to understand. If my niche is Silicon Valley singles looking for better relationships, I know *who* they are. Now I can rather easily find out *where* they are—and those are my channels. If they're online and members of an Internet community or forum, I can convey my marketing message through that channel. If they're listening to radio shows for singles, reading magazines for singles, attending clubs or outings for singles, and so on, again, I can focus my marketing through those channels.

Both of these informative aspects of your marketing—content and channel—come to light *through* your niche.

BENEFITS OF CHOOSING A NICHE

Stemming from our previous discussion, there are additional benefits to choosing a niche.

- **A niche guides you to follow your passion, which is fun!**

  Passion is the key to lasting business success; chasing money leads to burnout. When you choose a niche, you can focus on something that really matters to you; something that inspires you, even if it's difficult or challenging (for some people, it will be *because* their niche is difficult and challenging that it will be so attractive!). Furthermore, focusing on your passion helps you avoid focusing only on what you need to do to survive, or "make a living." The best way to identify what you're passionate about—and hence what your niche is—is to answer the question: *Would you do this for free?* If the answer is yes, then that could be a viable niche for you. If the answer is no . . . then keep looking!

- **A niche enables you to be creative.**

  As discussed earlier, focusing on a niche is not limiting; it only seems that way in a superficial sense. But once you dive into your niche, you'll discover just how many creative opportunities lie open to you. Suddenly, and often when you're not even

80

thinking about your niche, your practice, or anything to do with your coaching at all, your intuition will supply you with a creative idea—an aha moment that will fuel your creative spirit. This happened to me when I started diving into relationship coaching. The idea that tapped into me—I won't say that I tapped into *it* since this came out of intuition—was Conscious Dating. Through that intuitive gift, I've created all kinds of services, products, and programs.

- **A niche helps you to be of service.**

  Obviously, even without a niche, coaches will help people; I'm not implying that *only* a coach with a niche will be helpful. However, I am confidently saying that a niche really helps you make a deep impact on a part of the society that is simply not being served as effectively as it deserves. A niche helps you cultivate an ongoing helpful contribution to a particular group or segment of society. And as a coach, you can humbly feel inspired that you're taking a leadership role in helping those people. In my world, I can say calmly and without hubris that I make a *huge* contribution to singles. I'm able to be of service to them outside of my office, nationally, internationally, now and for the foreseeable future.

- **A niche helps you create a legacy.**

  Through the products, services, programs, and packages that you create for your niche, you will also create a legacy that will outlive you (not to be morbid or anything, but you know what I mean). For example, Conscious Dating is a registered trademark. So all of the intellectual property protected by that trademark—the program, the books, the workbooks, the tools, and the strategies—are going to survive me. I can sell them, will them to my kids, donate them . . . it's up to me. A niche helps tie everything together.

- **A niche is more profitable and lends itself to multiple income streams.**

  Many people choose not to pursue a niche because they think it would lead to *less* income potential; but this is short-term thinking. When you identify and target your niche, you actually position yourself to make more income over the long term, because you're effectively bridging the gap between what you do (your specialization) and whom you help (your niche). You can focus more effectively on both the content and the channel (as described earlier), and you can also create all kinds of products, programs, and packages that are anchored by your niche. In my experience, for example, I went from scratch to having programs for singles, conducting seminars for singles, hosting gatherings for singles, training other people to work with singles and licensing them to use my programs, writing a book, selling books, having workbooks, and producing professional manuals. Whenever I do a seminar I record it, and the recording becomes another product. On and on and on and on.

CHOOSING A NICHE

Now that you're (one hopes) open to the idea of identifying a niche for your practice, the next step is actually choosing the right one for you. I've identified 11 strategies for choosing a niche.

1. **The mirror strategy.** Birds of a feather aren't the only creatures that flock together; people do, too. So the mirror strategy is all about looking in the mirror and choosing a niche of people *who are like you*. Indeed, this may seem strange because as a therapist, you're not used to identifying yourself with clients in this way. But as a coach, remember, you'll be dealing with functional, healthy people who want to be more functional and healthy. Identifying with them is not only easy, but it's inspiring, too. The strategy here is to identify some key points of similarity between you and the people you want to serve. If you're a somewhat geeky engineer type, then those are possibly the kinds of people you'll be able to serve best. Not only will you have some insights into their world views and the challenges they face, but you'll also be able to establish rapport quickly—perhaps immediately—because that similarity will resonate in you and the people you help.

2. **The calling strategy.** Ask yourself: Whom do I feel called to help? Go beyond the *how* of this answer, and try to tap into the *who*. Don't worry or be bogged down by the practical (or what seem like practical) obstacles. For example, if you don't know where on earth you'd find the people you're called to help, don't let that throw cold water on your enthusiasm. You'll have time to explore the practical aspects of your potential niche later. For now, just listen to the stillness inside you and really try to detect who it is you feel called to help. The answer may surprise you, maybe even shock you. That's okay. Chances are it won't be what you expect!

3. **The testimonial strategy.** Now this is a fun strategy. What do people, especially your clients, say about you? Try to identify any themes that *other people* notice more clearly than you do. For example, you may not even realize that your sense of humor is something that your clients or friends love about you and value highly. Might that mean you'll coach entertainers or public speakers? Or perhaps you'll see that many testimonials—too many to be a coincidence—point out that you're gifted at putting them at ease and making them feel calm and focused. Perhaps that means you'll coach elite athletes and other peak performers. Feel free to ask for specific feedback from your friends or clients if that helps. For example, you may want to ask: "Are there three qualities about me that you value or find helpful?"

4. **The attraction strategy.** What and whom are you attracted to, and just as important—if not *more* important—what is attracted to you (whether you want it to be or not)? An example from my life may help you understand this strategy better. In private practice, I started attracting a number of recovering alcoholics. Now, I'm not an alcoholic and have never been one. Furthermore, I've never been addicted to anything, and have never therefore been in recovery or rehab. Now, on the surface, I could have (and admittedly, I did at first) assume that my calling was to work with individuals and couples dealing with addiction. But then I started to pay more attention to this phenomenon, and I discovered that the majority of these recovering alcoholics wanted to work on their *relationships* with me,

not their addictions. I had to ask myself silently: Why me? It didn't matter that I had no expertise in addictions. This niche *found me* on its own. Life does that. It doesn't require permission.

5. **The life story strategy.** Ask yourself: In your life story, what tragedies have you overcome? What peak experiences have you enjoyed? Carefully and as objectively as you can, *witness* your life story as if it were happening to someone else, or you were watching it on television. A great exercise is to create a time line from birth to the present with all the significant events you can recall. By paying attention to some key events in your life, you may stumble upon a niche that was simply waiting patiently to be discovered. For example, when I was a child, my dad—who is an artist—used to take me to marinas and paint scenes of boats, especially sailboats. He often talked to the skippers, and sometimes they'd invite us to go for a little sail. As an adult I learned how to sail and have owned several sailboats. To this day, whenever I see a sailboat or I talk to somebody who owns a sailboat, I get excited and happy. Now, where's the niche value here? I could be a coach for sailors! Just by reviewing my life story, I'm able to easily pick out a niche possibility. It really is that simple.

6. **The serendipity strategy.** Sometimes, positive stuff will just happen on its own, without (and sometimes despite) your involvement. And if you pay attention, it's entirely possible (why not?) that this is a message to you that is worthy of heeding. Here's an undeniably serendipitous example from my life. When I was practicing therapy, I published a column in a local parents' magazine in my area. A social worker at a local hospital read one of my columns and invited me to give a presentation to her "new moms" group at the hospital. I was happy to do so, and gave my talk—and then another one, since the first one was so warmly received. My expectation was simply to be of service to these new moms and possibly to get some referrals for my practice. But what ended up happening was that this social worker became the biggest referral source I've ever had! It almost was like every stressed-out new mom and every marriage that was having trouble that went through that hospital was referred to

my office. I could have easily developed a whole specialized niche around couples having difficulty adjusting to parenthood. The same thing can happen to you (and probably does all the time). Pay attention to those intuitive coincidences. Your niche could be waiting to reveal itself to you, if you're simply willing to be open to it.

7. **The pipeline strategy.** It may help you to envision your niche as a series of stages, instead of a single, static thing. For example, my work with singles is a *great* pipeline strategy because they become couples, get married, have children, sometimes get divorced, the children grow up, get married, have children, and so on. So there's a huge pipeline there that starts with singles. All of those people become potential clients. This is very different than, say, being a hypnotherapist who helps people quit smoking. Once they quit, that's it: the end. There's no pipeline, unless, possibly, they want to quit other harmful things. But really, if the entire marketing strategy is built around quitting smoking, the pipeline ends when they quit smoking. So if you have a variety of niches in mind, think about which one has a longer life span and can lead to multiple contacts with the same client.

8. **The gateway strategy.** Similar to the pipeline strategy, the gateway strategy asks: What is the most successful gateway into your practice? What is the path of least resistance, the groups of people you can reach the most easily? Answering this question is why my niche is singles instead of couples: because singles are simply so much easier to target than couples. Frankly, in my experience couples are not motivated to hire anybody to help them with their relationship until and unless they're in serious trouble! Of course I want to work with couples, but for my marketing, singles who want healthy, positive relationships are much easier to find and are more motivated and open to coaching. So when you're thinking of your niche, determine which one will be easiest to reach.

9. **The replication strategy.** Ask yourself: What niche is most easily replicable? What can you just do over, and over, and over again? There is an echo of the pipeline strategy here. The best niches are those that don't become smaller the more people you help. For example,

think of smokers. Paradoxically, the more smokers you help, the fewer there are! With Vietnam War veterans or survivors of 9/11, eventually you'll be out of business because there will be fewer and fewer potential clients over time. So focus on a niche that has increasing enrollment—where more people are continually being added to the pool of potential clients.

10. **The unmet need strategy.** Take a look around and ask: What unmet needs are there? As bizarre as it may sound, many niches remain unexplored and underserved simply because specialists overlook this strategy. When I became a coach I decided that I wanted to help singles. And thanks to my market research I found that this market had clear unmet needs: They wanted and didn't have a safe, fun, and educational place to meet other singles. So, guess what? That's what I created for them and offered to them in my advertising. And it worked beyond anything I imagined, simply because I targeted an unmet need. In this way, I didn't have to invent *anything*. I simply had to observe, identify, and innovate.

11. **The quick-start strategy.** This is very simple! From a practical standpoint, ask yourself: What can you launch the fastest? What do you have the most contacts for? What do you have the most in place for? What can you just get started quickly doing *now*? This is the strategy that I suggest you use when transitioning from a job to private practice. Indeed, you have to survive before you can thrive. And I have seen a lot of practitioners bomb because they had (and have) unrealistic expectations. The quick-start strategy is the shortest route you can identify from A to B. It gets you off the ground. Now, you might be thinking: *Doesn't this strategy conflict with the calling strategy discussed earlier?* No, it doesn't. You can and should identify and build your niche based on your calling; if you don't, then you'll just burn out anyway, regardless of how successful you are. The quick-start strategy is merely a way to get you moving forward—to get you providing coaching—so that you can maintain and grow your practice. Frankly, if you're unable to pay the rent for next month, or have a website built or do any of the other things you need to run your practice, you won't even have a niche to worry about—because you won't have a practice.

How to Own Your Niche

What does "owning your niche" mean? It doesn't necessarily mean having a monopoly or so much market share that you're essentially the only game in town (or state or country). True, while it's possible that you may be the pioneer of your niche, that won't last—your very success will invite competition. And this is not a bad thing, provided that the niche in the first place is not so thin and underpopulated that a few new entrants will mean a catfight for a limited, dwindling supply of prospective clients. Fortunately, you won't run into this problem, because one of your criteria for choosing a niche will be its pipeline strategy (future opportunities generated by a single client), and another is the replication strategy (more people continually being added to the pool of potential clients). "Owning your niche" means that you become the go-to person for your niche; you become so accomplished and well-known among the people in your niche that you become their preferred provider, and most referrals and media inquiries related to your niche come your way.

Owning your niche can be both easy and fun, and involves seven clear steps: market research, pilot project, branding, service delivery, niche communities, group services, and leveraging.

Market Research

I cannot overstate the value of doing market research. In fact, along with a few other key factors, credible market research is what differentiates successful practitioners from unsuccessful practitioners (or, if you like, practitioners in business and practitioners not in business). Market research starts with learning core relevant facts about your niche clients. Who are they? Where are they? What do they want? What works for them? What *doesn't* work for them? How are they being served (if at all) by other services?

Ultimately, you want your market research to help you create a profile of your *ideal client*. And by *ideal* I don't mean the nicest or the one who will send you the most referrals because you helped in such wonderful ways. Sure, that's ideal, but not in the sense that it's being used here. Rather, you want to clearly picture who it is that you're serving. You want to understand what motivates them and what doesn't, what they're striving for, what they consider success to be (because it may not be the same as what you think it is, or even what you think it *should* be), and so on.

Quality market research is done through one-to-one conversations with people who fit your niche, or through a focus group. And let me say bluntly that surveys are useless, especially e-mail or online surveys sent to a large group. The information you receive won't help you. Your goal is to learn about your niche clients from the *inside out* and get to know them so well that it becomes clear how to market to them and what services to provide. E-mail and online surveys won't do this.

Ideally, you'll conduct market research continuously on your existing programs, new programs, ideas for programs, and so on. Just as large corporations use market research to effectively market to and serve their customers, this is a key to your success.

Here are five steps for conducting market research:

Step 1: Research your niche for their demographic information, other professionals and organizations that serve them, other approaches to helping them, websites, online social networking groups, books, workshops, and so on. Call or meet with similar and complementary professionals and organizations to learn more about how they help the people in your niche. Do your homework and become an expert on available information about your target clients.

Step 2: Put together some ideas for programs, branding, services, and so on. Come up with a variety of program names to find out which they prefer. A great exercise is to brainstorm answers to this question: "If I were to write a book or deliver a workshop for my niche, what would I call it?"

Step 3: Identify three to five people who fit your niche. Ideally, these are people you know. If not, then ask your network for referrals. Contact them for informational interviews.

Step 4: Conduct your informational interviews and ask for feedback about your ideas from step 2. Ask what they read, where they hang out, what groups and organizations they join, what publications they subscribe to, and so on. Ask them about their experiences, needs, goals, and challenges. Ask them about what they've done, where they've gone, and whom they've worked with to get support for the need or goal you will address in your coaching practice. Listen *very* closely to the language they use to describe their needs and goals. Ask for their top three problems and top three goals. Ask them to describe their ideal support service or program to address each need or goal.

Step 5: Compile your data and ideas, and use them to design the services, branding, and programs for your niche. Follow up with your market research participants and get their feedback on your ideas, and ask them for referrals as well. Remember: An important principle is that people support what they help create, and when you follow up with those who helped you along the way, you'll be pleasantly surprised by their excitement and support. In fact, a common and delightful by-product is that some of them might sign up for your program!

Pilot Project

This comes *after* your market research—not before (something that a number of practitioners mistakenly do). Based on your market research, create a test program to see how things go. What kind of feedback are you getting? Is your market research accurate? Is your niche well-defined? Use all of the feedback you get—spoken and unspoken, positive and negative—to further refine your market research. If you want, you can even offer your pilot project for free, though I urge you to carefully market this so that you don't create unrealistic expectations among the participants/clients who may eventually sign up for your services. Of course, you may want to offer them a discounted rate for being so helpful to you at this stage of your practice, which is something I recommend.

Branding

Your brand identity is what you are communicating—actively, passively, directly, and indirectly—about you, your practice, and your services. Everything *feeds* into the brand, from the name itself to its imaging, to the policies that you create, to the location of your practice. A word of caution: Don't hide behind your brand. It drives me crazy when practitioners market themselves, have a sophisticated website, and I can't find out who they are, what they look like, or even if they're a person or some entity. As a coach, you want a strong brand that conveys a *strong presence*. Now, this doesn't mean that your website and other marketing collateral should be all about you. That kind of self-promotion is another thing that drives me crazy. Simply, you want to make it easy for prospective clients to learn about you, how you can help, and other key things that appeal to common sense. Also remember that your branding must reflect and convey your niche — that is, the people you're helping. You want to demonstrate that you understand their needs and aspirations, and are capable of helping them achieve their goals (more about branding in Chapter 7).

Service Delivery

If you enter a restaurant, everything the restaurant offers is on a menu. You have the beverage category over here, you have the appetizers over there, and the desserts are on the back. And it's up to you, the customer, to flip through and select what you want. Now, for restaurants, this is fine. For a coaching practice, it's not. Obliging clients to "create their own meal" by picking and choosing services that you offer is burdensome and unpleasant. The way to avoid this is to design a service delivery system that conveniently ushers your clients through your service offerings. Think of it as a kind of curriculum. You start at A, you go to B, then to C, and so on, until they graduate (and possibly become coaches themselves!). Also keep in mind that your service delivery options must make sense for the people in your niche. Don't just throw numbers at them — like "two sessions a month for $200, four sessions a month for $350" and so on. Instead, focus on what you're offering, and the outcomes of those offerings. Your clients can then make an informed decision on what to buy.

As an example, my services for singles in Silicon Valley started with a weekly safe, fun, and educational singles event on Friday evenings called the Friday Night Social. Participants were then invited to join our Conscious Dating classes and workshops. Graduates of those classes and workshops were invited to join an ongoing coaching support group. And when participants appeared to have a need that the coaching support group couldn't adequately meet, they were invited to meet for individual coaching.

The successful outcome of our coaching services and programs for singles was that they would enter into an exclusive relationship, at which time we would invite them to participate in our coaching program for precommitted and premarital couples. And once they became committed, we would invite them to participate in our coaching program for committed couples.

Host a Niche Community

We survive and thrive in relationships. We are social beings, and cannot be successful or happy alone. And in today's world, despite a ridiculous amount of technology that keeps us connected to each other, that need for community still prevails, as evidenced by the success of online social networking services such as Facebook and Twitter. As a coach, one of the noblest services that you can offer is simply to help the clients and prospects in your niche get together. Of course, you'll enjoy some benefits, too:

- *External marketing.* A niche community attracts people you don't know, who don't yet know you.
- *Internal marketing.* A niche community builds your relationships with your prospects so they hire you.
- *Low-cost marketing.* A niche community is a viable service that can pay for itself, and even generate a profit.
- *Stimulates word of mouth.* Participants in a niche community will more readily tell their friends about a community resource than a private (high-cost) service.
- *Helps build strategic alliances.* A niche community allows professionals to participate and cross-refer. For example, I invited my local Silicon Valley colleagues to give presentations to my community of singles, and in return they referred their clients and others to my niche community.

- *Increases visibility.* A niche community establishes you as the go-to resource associated with your niche.
- *Increases credibility.* The success of your niche community reflects upon your abilities as a service professional.
- *Increases effectiveness of service delivery system.* A niche community exposes more people to your various program options.
- *Increases traffic.* A niche community is a perfect opportunity to offer a free or low-cost gathering, which attracts more people and creates more prospects.
- *Attracts partners/collaborators.* A niche community brings together other like-minded professionals who will want to participate.
- *Transforms a practice into a business.* A niche community gives you the chance to promote multiple revenue streams that complement (or even become more predominant than) your one-on-one client work.

My weekly Friday Night Social for Silicon Valley singles became a true community of like-minded singles socializing and supporting each other. They helped run the programs, formed committees, went out for coffee as a group after each event, planned social activities together, and introduced each other to potential partners—all of which we supported and facilitated.

In return, participants in this community referred their friends, family, and coworkers, signed up for our programs, and were our biggest supporters. We took good care of them, and they took good care of us. This active community of conscious singles attracted numerous new participants each week who wanted to be part of such a positive and supportive environment that was unlike anything else they could find. Our classes, workshops, coaching groups, and programs were filled to capacity, and we added staff and grew quickly. While a weekly event such as this might seem labor intensive (who wants to work every Friday night?), it helped me build a wildly successful coaching business in a very short time.

What kinds of niche communities can you create? There are some options:

- **In person.** Draw from your local community and meet in person. This is the optimal choice if you deliver your services in person as I did in Silicon Valley.
- **Virtual.** Meet online and/or by telephone, and draw from anywhere in the world. This is best when you combine your e-mail distribution list with regular conference calls.
- **Open membership.** Anyone can join.
- **Restricted membership.** Members are screened and must meet certain criteria.
- **Free or fee.** Members can join for free or must pay. Often guests can attend on a trial basis and must pay to continue.

And last, here are some tips for creating a successful niche community:

- Define your niche clients and do your market research to identify what they want or need.
- Provide more value than expected.
- Be continuously creative and keep everything fun and interesting.
- Take responsibility for the leadership and outcome. Most communities fail due to lack of leadership.
- Involve participants—form committees, and ask for volunteers to greet, host, set up, break down, and so forth.
- Don't do it alone. Form a partnership, collaborate with other like-minded professionals, and outsource administrative functions to free you to work on your business and serve your clients.
- Form strategic alliances. Network with similar and complementary professionals and organizations.
- Create an organized system and plan events well ahead of time.
- Be responsive to participant issues and requests.
- Use a website, newsletter, schedule of future programs/events, e-mail distribution list, and conference calls to communicate with participants and prospects (and keep them engaged). Social networking websites make this easy, such as Facebook, Twitter, Meetup, Ning, and the like.

- Use a registration process—even for free events—which allows you to capture contact information to add to your database. An auto-responder subscription box on your website works well for this.
- Use short feedback forms to solicit input about events, with "Please contact me about . . ." with your calls to action at the bottom.
- Create safety by having and enforcing rules, such as this one from our singles community: "We reserve the right to refuse admission to anyone who does not meet our minimum standards of grooming, behavior, and sobriety."

Provide Group Services

This is the fastest way to private practice success. In my experience, going from meeting one client at a time on an hourly basis to meeting with groups (speaking to groups and offering group services, classes, workshops, teleclasses, conference calls, teleclinics, coaching groups, support groups, and so on) is a *very* effective way to develop and serve a niche. Not only does it enable you to serve more people, but it's also (obviously) more financially rewarding, too.

Leveraging Your Niche

As you grow your niche you build your platform. Why does this matter? Because your platform answers the questions: Who knows you? How many people know you? What do they say about you? What do you already have in place? And the better answers you have for these questions, the stronger your platform, and the more ownership you have of your niche (especially with the positive media attention that comes with this leverage). Here's a test: You probably have a good platform if you Google your name and find multiple references to your specialty and niche on the Internet.

CAN YOU COACH MORE THAN ONE NICHE IN YOUR PRACTICE?

Yes! By emphasizing the need to choose a niche, I don't want you to think that you can have only one. In fact, you can serve as many niches as you want and can handle. Often, you can leverage one niche to expand and serve another. For example, if my niche is Silicon Valley singles, I can use everything I have in place to serve singles of another geographical location or create an online community of singles for a virtual practice.

Think of it this way: Each niche is a separate line of business with its own audience, marketing channels, priorities, and so on. In my practice building programs, I recommend focusing on one niche exclusively for three to six months before adding another niche. This allows your practice to organically grow and develop, building a solid foundation of financial security for your business. It also helps you avoid the mistake of overextending and trying to do too much for too many.

Designing Your Service Delivery System

How to use market research to guarantee your success.
Designing a service delivery system to meet the needs of your niche.
How to create packages, programs, and products for your niche.

In Chapter 5, we covered choosing a niche, niche marketing, and how to own your niche. We also looked at how you can have multiple niches, which might be a relief to you if you're one of many therapists who resist the idea of choosing a niche as too restrictive and limiting.

Here in Chapter 6, we bring niche marketing down to earth to the practical level of how you design and deliver your services for a successful coaching business.

SURFACING YOUR SERVICE DELIVERY SYSTEM

Some therapists balk at the idea of being "in business." That is, they prefer to see what they do as strictly a helping service and consider business to be antithetical to helping clients. This view is curiously naive and, while that alone wouldn't merit criticism in this book (this isn't about therapists and why they do curiously naive things), that flawed perspective *does* need to be identified and removed if the transition to coaching is going to be successful and smooth.

Here's why: As a therapist, you've relied on *something* in the background and out of the way to generate clients and, quite frankly, stay in business (there's that awful b-word again!). That *something* brought your service to the attention of your clients. That *something* positioned you to be paid for your services. And *something* repeated this process so that you could continue doing it.

All of those *something*s put together comprise your service delivery system, though you may not have viewed your practice in these terms. You don't need to know how gravity works in order to take a successful flight. Similarly, as a therapist, you (likely) don't need to know how your service delivery system works in order to remain gainfully employed. You can have a casual understanding of it, but that's really all you need. Other people and groups — insurance companies, regulatory boards, and so on — create the service delivery system for you. You simply have to find your place within it and do your thing, and you get to be a paid, successful therapist. In a way, in a traditional one-to-one practice, you could argue that there is no system at all; it's just service delivery. That is, you deliver your service and that's the end of it. The other parts are governed by other people and groups. It's nice and simple that way, which is one reason many therapists remain therapists long after they've burned out.

As a coach, things change a bit. Those helpful groups that provided you with ready-to-treat clients and further ensured that you'd be paid aren't there anymore. The onus is now on *you* to create a service delivery system that reaches out to your target market, ushers prospects into your practice, and positions both them and you for a successful coaching experience that results in you making a good living as a coach.

BUILDING YOUR SERVICE DELIVERY SYSTEM

With all of this having been said, building your service delivery system is not odious, unpleasant, or even undeservedly challenging. You don't have to invest thousands of dollars or hundreds of hours. Your focus simply needs to be on understanding how to *funnel* the right kind of people into your practice (and by "right kind," I mean the kinds of people who are going to benefit from your targeted coaching services *and* who are going to pay for them).

So how do you build this thing? Start with this principle, and please, please, *please* never forget it—because doing so is expensive and often perilous for a practice, particularly a new one: Your service delivery system *responds* to your market research; it doesn't *dictate* your service delivery.

Let me dig deeper. It's efficient, convenient, and psychologically satisfying—a *deadly* trio when it points the wrong way—to build a service delivery system around what sounds good or seems right to you. Regardless of how good your hunches are, or how many times in the past you've predicted what the marketplace would do, my unwavering advice to you is always to do your market research *first*, and then base your service delivery on the hard data that you generate. If this merely verifies what you already guessed, then more power to you; you're a divining rod for service delivery systems. But more times than not, your market research will reshape your hypotheses, if not outright obliterate them (a humbling, yet staggeringly informative experience).

Another way of remembering all of the preceding—a more fun, positive way—is simply this: *Market to your target audience, not to yourself*. And make no mistake: *You are not your target market*. This is one of the biggest flaws in all marketing (by no means limited to therapists or coaches). Often, businesses of all sizes forget that they *aren't* their target market. Or to put it differently: They assume that they *are* their target market. So they simply say to themselves: "Hey, this makes sense to me, so it must make sense to the people I'm trying to communicate with."

Guess what? This is rarely the case!

There are a couple of reasons for this, both of them strangely obvious when you write them out the way I will here.

First, your target market doesn't define what you do in *your* terms.

You live and breathe this stuff. You (naturally) take mental shortcuts. You know what your subject looks like from the inside. You know the details. Your target market, however, does *not*. Your prospective clients have some understanding, but not at your depth or with your breadth. And this difference is far, far more than just a matter of simplifying and avoiding deadly jargon. It's a fundamental shift in *what* you communicate, not just *how*.

For example, you may think that "coaching is a service that helps people achieve goals and move forward in their lives." Sure, that sounds reasonable. But if you ask 100 people out there what coaching means, less than 10%—probably less than 5%—will come even close to that definition. They'll more likely say something like, "Coaching is a way for me to overcome problems and be happy." The two versions—yours and theirs—may look fairly similar, but the differences speak volumes. You're looking at something from a feature-driven perspective. They're looking at things from a benefit-driven perspective. You're looking at something in terms of *what it does*—which is logical and factual. They're looking at it in terms of *how it promises to achieve a satisfying outcome*—which is emotional and abstract.

And keep in mind that this is just an example. If you go one step further and imagine what people in a targeted niche will say about coaching, the differences between your initial assumptions and their black-and-white responses will be even bigger. This is because your targeted clients have their own language and will interpret and define coaching as it relates to *their* world (that is, to their niche). In doing this, they'll change more than just your (expected) words around. They'll change the nuance and even the direction. What struck you as so obvious will reveal itself to be quite different. And you don't have to wait long to see the evidence. The moment you start generating market research data, the proof will be right there in front of you: What you *thought* they wanted isn't what they *actually do* want.

Another example of how you view things differently than others is in the concept of therapy itself. I'd argue that you believe, rationally, that pretty much everyone out there in the world would benefit from therapy and enjoy personal growth. But guess what? Most people out there will disagree! Instead, they'll figure that "someone has to be pretty messed up to need therapy" and that working with a therapist is a choice of last resort.

(And as an aside: Yes, this stigma about therapy pains many therapists, as it did me. And worse than that, it prevents therapists from reaching many of the people that they'd like to help. In fact, this dynamic may be one of the reasons you're looking to bring coaching into your professional world. If so, then be assured: You aren't alone. Welcome to the club!)

Second, you don't buy your own services.

As absurd as it seems just to blurt it out like that, it's the truth (and, yes, absurd, too). You don't buy coaching—at least not from yourself. And so, while you may have some powerful—and ultimately correct—insights about your target market, you truly cannot see their world as clearly as *they* can, because, again, you don't buy your own services.

Or to put it differently: You're already *sold* on your services. And whether or not you're consciously aware of it, your intuition and subconscious are working overtime, behind the scenes, to create the reality that you want to experience—that is, one where everyone loves your coaching and would buy it simply because, well, who wouldn't?

Remember: People don't always (some cynics might argue that they *often* don't) buy things that make sense. How many people smoke, even though they know it's doing severe damage to them? How many people crave losing weight but drive to restaurants where even the water has 1,000 calories? These people are not insane. Their minds are enabling them to do something patently *in*sensible, so that decisions like smoking, or speeding dangerously in a car, or eating that hot sauce that they *know* will have them crawling helplessly to the bathroom at 3 A.M. all, somehow, make sense.

The same unreasonable logic applies to your marketing. You cannot simply assume that people will come to you for coaching because they have problems and you have solutions. Yes, that would be why *you* would buy your services. But, as we absurdly pointed out, *you* don't buy your services. So that means you need to understand both the problems and the solutions in *their* terms. And those terms are invariably going to be different in small and surprisingly big ways.

Alas, I can wrap all of this up by simply saying this: If you ignore (or don't conduct) your market research and simply put together what you want to do or what you assume is going to work, then you risk failure. If you listen and respond to what your niche wants and needs, you are almost guaranteed success.

YOUR SERVICE DELIVERY SYSTEM AS A CLIENT CREATION FUNNEL

You may have come across the term *marketing funnel*, which is a way to easily represent a system of reaching out to a target market and bringing prospects into your sales cycle. Or to put this into coaching

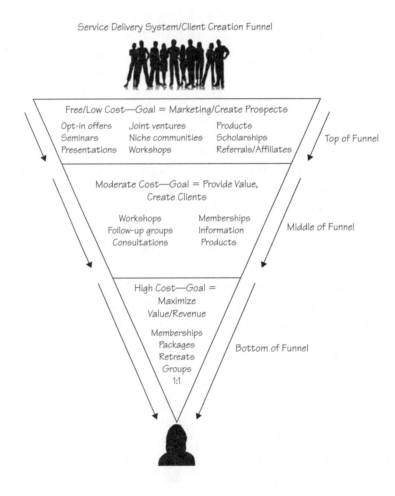

Service Delivery System/Client Creation Funnel

Free/Low Cost—Goal = Marketing/Create Prospects

Opt-in offers	Joint ventures	Products
Seminars	Niche communities	Scholarships
Presentations	Workshops	Referrals/Affiliates

Top of Funnel

Moderate Cost—Goal = Provide Value, Create Clients

Workshops	Memberships
Follow-up groups	Information
Consultations	Products

Middle of Funnel

High Cost—Goal = Maximize Value/Revenue

Memberships
Packages
Retreats
Groups
1:1

Bottom of Funnel

terms: It's a way of reaching out to the people in your niche who will benefit from your coaching, and of introducing them to your services, ushering them into your practice, and ultimately turning them into paying, satisfied clients.

Here is a snapshot of a three-tiered client creation funnel. Don't worry if these terms make little or no sense at this point. I'll explore each tier, and you'll see how it all fits together. For now, just become comfortable (or as comfortable as you can be) with the *shape* of the client creation funnel: The widest part is at top, and the narrowest is down at the bottom (this is sometimes called an "upside-down pyramid" by marketing types).

The top tier of this funnel consists of your marketing activities designed to create prospects. The middle tier contains low- to moderate-cost products and group services designed to provide value and create clients. The bottom tier is where your client services live.

TOP OF FUNNEL: YOUR MARKETING ACTIVITIES

One of the wonders of marketing is that it allows you to communicate with people you don't even know—people who, potentially, are searching for precisely what you have to offer. And it's the mission of your marketing activities (the top of your funnel) to reach out to these good people and say: *"Hi there, I exist."*

While there are many ways to do this, the strategy that I use—and hence endorse—is one where you market by providing value. That is, it is where you share valuable information and resources with your niche prospects in a way that encourages them to want more.

There are three very important things to note about these kinds of "marketing by providing value" activities:

First, they're free.

If you *must* charge something (and I have a hard time imagining that you *must*, but maybe you do), then it should just offset your costs, not be a source of profit. Remember, these activities are about reaching out into your niche and introducing yourself. Just as you wouldn't charge someone for simply meeting you for the first time on the street, at a conference, or even in your office, you shouldn't charge for these kinds of marketing activities. Frankly, most people won't pay, and even a nominal fee will turn away far more people than it will attract. In the bigger picture, you'll undermine your marketing and will lose money.

Second, they must be valuable.

This second point seems obvious, but it has to be mentioned. The resources you offer must be perceived as *valuable* to your niche. So that means they can't be thinly veiled advertising where you just self-promote and pitch your services. A resource has to be something that your niche finds interesting, informative, and helpful. Really, the easiest way to determine whether something is valuable is to put yourself in your prospective client's shoes. Would *you* find the resource valuable? Would it help you learn something useful, or provide you with a tool or insight that you'd be glad to receive? Your market research should help you identify your niche's top needs, challenges, goals, and questions, which you can use to create free products (e-book, booklet, audio recording, CD, etc.) and programs (seminar, e-course, teleclass, etc.) of high perceived value that will attract prospective clients.

Third, they're designed to build a relationship.

What you offer at this stage is not the be-all and end-all of how you hope to connect with your niche. It's not the end of the line; rather, it's the beginning. As such, create your resources with a vision toward encouraging prospective clients to *deepen* their relationship with you—and move further down the sales funnel. One of the most powerful ways to do this is simply to have their next step planned and a strong, focused website for that next step that you can point people toward at the end of your report or e-book, or mention in your audio program, or highlight in your presentations.

Examples of Top-of-Funnel Marketing Activities

You've probably come across some (or all) of these types of top-of-funnel resources in your own travels. They include offering a newsletter, a seminar, or a teleclass; downloading an audio; and so on.

In addition, there are what I'd call more primary forms of top-of-funnel marketing activities, which are aimed at, simply, communicating what you *do*. These primary types are: networking, speaking, and writing.

Networking   Networking includes building your referral relationships and joint venture partnerships. It also includes participating in groups and organizations that fit your niche (online and offline). Research shows that by far the most effective way for private-practice professionals to find new clients is by word-of-mouth referral. Networking and building your referral relationships form the single most effective way to fill your practice. I discuss this further in Chapter 7.

Speaking   Speaking refers to giving presentations to groups, either in person or via conference call (teleclass or teleseminar). Speaking is very effective for both coaches and therapists, as it gives listeners an experience of your presence and voice that approximates your actual service. Listeners connect with your voice and message and become attracted to the idea of working with you. The listening experience is also safe for your listeners because they're anonymous or part of a group, and are thus not on the hot seat in a one-to-one conversation. They can experience you from a distance and become comfortable with you.

As a nice residual benefit, your speaking engagements can be recorded (audio or video), and repurposed into programs available on your website. You can then offer these programs to website visitors in exchange for their e-mail addresses (this is called generating an opt-in, because people are actively and directly opting to be on your mailing list). And even better, you can set this up so that it's automatic—you don't have to manually send your website visitors anything. They'll simply self-identify that they want to opt in to get your audio or video program, and they'll automatically receive the material.

Writing   Writing includes all of the content on your website, your blog, published articles (in print and online), any books or e-books that you write, e-programs you might have (these are a series of lessons delivered automatically by an autoresponder), and so on. Through your writing you'll provide valuable information to engage, inform, and help the people in your niche see that you're a credible expert who understands their needs.

Also, when writing (and this applies to speaking, too), don't worry about giving too much information away and, ironically, not positioning yourself to actually coach these people. Information in today's world is freely and easily available. The information that you provide will motivate and inspire, but by itself won't typically create change—which is why they need you (and by all means, you can convey this in clear, honest terms in your material).

If you're willing and able, I recommend you consider writing a book. You have information and wisdom to share, and if you write a book that targets your niche it will be your best door opener and marketing tool. I resisted the call to write a book for a long time, but in retrospect wish that I had started years ago. Don't worry (as I did) that you might not have anything unique to say; just write from your experience and perspective, and in doing so you'll provide value to people in your niche.

Products   Both free and low-cost products are valuable marketing tools at the top of your funnel. These include audio and video programs; e-books and e-programs; and printed materials such as books, pamphlets, miniposters, and wallet cards. All of these products can be produced digitally and offered online at virtually no cost to you. Hard copies can be produced in bulk at very low cost to be distributed in person or by mail.

Don't be afraid to invest some money in creating a great promotional product, as most of them are far less costly than a color brochure—and are more effective! For example, the last time I used brochures (four-color trifold on glossy card stock) I paid close to $2.50 each, but a promotional CD cost me 40 cents each, and the CD is *far* more effective at providing value, attracting prospects, and delivering my message and promotional information.

Workshops and seminars Workshops and seminars are very effective for attracting prospective clients. While you *could* provide these at a low cost to cover your expenses, I recommend offering them for free, provided that attendees register in advance on your website (again, you can use an autoresponder system to make this fast and easy for everyone, including you). Again, don't balk at the idea of offering something for free. Many successful personal growth gurus conduct free seminars and workshops as their primary marketing activity. Why? Because until people get to know you, a fee can be an impenetrable barrier. Remember: You're not at the bottom of your marketing funnel yet. That means you don't need to (and shouldn't expect to or design your services to) profit from these top-of-funnel activities. This is all about generating prospects by reaching out and saying hello; it's not about generating revenues . . . yet!

Niche communities We covered this topic in Chapter 5 (so if you skipped Chapter 5, guess what your homework is!). Frankly, niche communities are my favorite top-of-funnel marketing activities. They're a gift that keeps on giving, and have worked very, very well for me (which means they can work for you, too).

MIDDLE OF FUNNEL: CLIENT ENROLLMENT ACTIVITIES

Middle-of-funnel activities allow you to connect with *many* potential clients, so that you can engage them individually and identify needs, goals, and challenges that require more focused, personalized support. Your middle-of-funnel target market is fed by your top-of-funnel activities.

Middle-of-funnel activities are low- to moderate-cost products, services, and programs designed to provide value, generate revenue, and (what is most important) create clients. Here's where you do more than just say hello; it's where you say: "I can help you, here's how, and here's what it will cost." As with your top-of-funnel activities, these address the needs of your niche that you identified in your market research.

Examples of Middle-of-Funnel Activities

Workshops, seminars, and classes Workshops, seminars, and classes are time-limited group programs that give participants (i.e., your potential clients) an *extensive* experience of you, so that when those activities are finished, there is a reasonable expectation that some or all of the participants will want to purchase your services and therefore become clients.

Unlike the top-of-funnel workshops and seminars that we looked at just a moment ago, here in the middle-of-funnel stage you're more direct and explicit about how your services are going to help participants. That's because at this stage of the funnel, it's very easy and natural (i.e., not sales-y) to discuss your offerings, and how, by working closely with you, participants can apply what they're learning — instead of struggling to do that on their own. Your participants have qualified themselves as very interested (hot prospects, in marketing lingo) in your coaching services, because they've paid real money and invested a significant chunk of time to participate in your workshop, seminar, or class. In other words, you know they're not lookie loos like some of the top-of-funnel folks. These people seriously want the results and benefits that you've made available, and they're willing to pay for them.

Paid information products Information products such as books, CDs, DVDs, e-books, and so on can be packaged into a home study program, which includes a workbook. What distinguishes these from the top-of-funnel products is that there should be a fee associated with them. These products can be digitized and offered as downloadable products from your website, which is good for immediate delivery and keeps your costs down. If you aren't sure what to put into your program, simply record the seminars, workshops, and other programs discussed in the preceding section.

The great thing about information products is that folks on the receiving end are telling you, clearly, that they're motivated to learn more about your services. Therefore, you definitely want to follow up and call or e-mail them. You can do this in a pleasant and acceptable way by simply thanking them for their order and letting them know that you're available for questions. You can also send them a gift certificate for a free consultation with you, or some other valuable incentive.

Also, it's a good idea to follow up a couple of weeks after the information product has been downloaded or shipped. This is because most purchasers of informational products don't get around to actually using them for a while. In my experience, when you contact folks and remind them of the value of consuming what they've already purchased, they respond favorably, and are very impressed by your caring customer service. As your business grows, I recommend that you add staff who can perform this important follow-up function.

Paid memberships Memberships include telephone and Web-based niche communities and both virtual and in-person group programs. The difference between the top-of-funnel niche communities and the middle-of-funnel niche communities is that here you provide more focused and personal support, coaching, and mentoring at a group level—and you'll charge enough to obtain participant commitment and investment. Also, a top-of-funnel niche community might have a casual "show up when you want" attitude, while this middle-of-funnel membership program expects regular participation, is ongoing, and uses recurring billing to charge by the month (or year) until the participant cancels.

A straightforward way to set up a middle-of-funnel membership program looks like this:

- Market the program with a promotional seminar or teleseminar.
- Begin the program with a six-week class to cover the information that members need to have and help them get started.
- Meet by telephone for ongoing support once or twice a month.

- Supplement the program with a dedicated website, an online community for group interaction, and regular teleclinics for more focused support and problem solving.
- Offer bonus seminars for more advanced information.

If you decide to run this kind of membership program virtually (i.e., online), you can potentially serve hundreds, even *thousands* of participants at the same time!

Bottom of Funnel: Your Client Services

The ultimate goal of your funnel is to create a regular stream of coaching clients. As a therapist you know that growth and change is hard, and that the vast majority of people need personal support to achieve their goals. It's exactly the same with coaching: Change is tough, but you can help. Your top- and middle-of-funnel activities introduce your prospective clients to this fact and convince them of it, and your bottom-of-funnel activities focus on carrying it out.

Examples of Bottom-of-Funnel Client Services

Individual coaching   Individual coaching might be the ultimate goal of your funnel system. However, if you successfully target your niche and develop solid top- and middle-of-funnel activities using the previously noted strategies and ideas, then you might encounter one of those nice problems to have: You don't have time to meet with individual clients! To remedy this, you can leverage your time with group coaching programs (this is discussed next). You can also bring associates into your organization, whom you train and mentor. You then choose the clients you want to coach, and refer the rest to your associates.

Group coaching   Group coaching is a great bottom-of-funnel activity, especially in a small group of 5 to 10. That's because it's affordable for participants, profitable for you, and very effective for achieving measurable coaching results. Participants benefit from multiple sources of input and support through brainstorming, masterminding, and coaching each other—provided that a good group leader is there to encourage and facilitate this. And as an added benefit, a good, ongoing coaching group becomes very tight-knit, which in turn functions as a powerful support system for participants that promotes longevity and retention; I've seen coaching groups stay together for years at a time.

Retreats Retreats are like workshops, though typically longer, more personalized, and more intimate; they are held in beautiful vacation-like settings, and often involve recreation and play in addition to "work." Imagine the great group coaching and transformational experiences you could provide with a small group in Hawaii, or on a cruise ship, or at a cabin in the mountains for a weekend or even a week or more!

Packages Packages involve grouping your services, products, and programs into an assortment tailored to meet the needs of your niche. All of the bottom-of-funnel client services we've looked at so far can be packaged and further grouped into tiers, such as "Silver," "Gold," and "Platinum" packages. To figure out how to do this, once you've designed your service delivery system and all of its components, ask yourself: "If a client were to pay top dollar for my best and most effective program, what would that program look like and how much would it cost?" Include all of your products, services, and programs, and provide numerous bonus items for added value (such as an iPod or MP3 player loaded with your audio programs, additional coaching/consulting time with partners or associates, free airfare and lodging for your retreats, and so on). To make smaller or less premium packages, simply start removing some of the pieces of the best package and reprice accordingly.

Remember: Although marketing and delivering free and low-cost products and programs (in the top and middle tiers of your funnel) might seem to require a lot of time and effort, and even some financial costs, the rewards are immense. You'll identify and connect with many highly qualified prospective clients—people you *couldn't* have reached otherwise.

LEVERAGING YOUR TIME AND BOOSTING YOUR INCOME

If you build a strong service delivery system by using some or even all of the activities suggested, you'll attract far, *far* more prospective clients than through a traditional practice. However, that can be a challenge in itself, because you may quickly find that you don't have enough time to absorb the demand. As mentioned, this is a nice problem to have, but it's nevertheless a problem that needs to be solved. Here are some key strategies that will help you leverage your time and boost your income:

Use Monthly Recurring Credit Card Billing

Through monthly recurring credit card billing, your clients make the buying decision once and momentum keeps them in your system until they make the decision and take the action to stop. Make sure to set up your individual and group coaching, memberships, and packages on monthly recurring credit card billing. You might consider a higher enrollment fee up front to get commitment, then an affordable monthly fee for ongoing participation (like a health club!).

Group Services

Group services are the key to a wildly successful practice where you *don't* run into brick walls because you don't have the time to meet each client one-on-one. Workshops, classes, seminars, and groups might be alien to you in your therapy practice, and you might hesitate and say, "But, David, I'm not good in front of a group." My answer? Nonsense! Just start small, and then work your way up to larger groups. In doing so (trust me), you'll serve many more people, make a significant difference in the world, and generate far more income that you could otherwise. And besides, groups are fun!

Hire Staff

Getting help is key to leveraging your time and income. Most coaches and therapists work alone, but to build a successful coaching practice, you will need staff who will enable you to focus your efforts on activities you do best and are the most profitable for you. The time you spend working on your own website, doing your own bookkeeping, mailing your own product orders, and so on may be interesting (though not always!), but it will bog you down and prevent your business from growing.

A Final Note on What *Not* to Do With Your Service Delivery System

Most of us enjoy pursuing our various professional interests and passions, but I caution you against trying to mash them all together to try to create a system from them—because the thing that will keep your system going is that it's *for your niche*, not for you.

For example, years ago I grew excited about the idea of putting on a workshop about fathering. I spent weeks researching, designing, and putting together materials. I called the workshop "Fatherhood in the '90s," and marketed it to my current clients, former clients, mailing list, referral sources, local men's and women's groups, and so on. It was a great workshop and was very well received, plus I really enjoyed teaching it. But when it was over, I put it on the shelf and never did it again.

Looking back, I kick myself about the lost opportunities from not following up this workshop. If I had asked myself "What's next?" after the workshop (or even better, *before* the workshop), I could have conducted it quarterly as a pipeline for potential clients. Or I could have followed it up with an ongoing support group for fathers. But I went back to my practice and absorbed myself in my work with my clients, paperwork, billing, and so on.

Why did this happen? Because, honestly, "Fatherhood in the '90s" was really for me—not for my niche. Once it was out of my system, so to speak, I lost interest, and it fizzled and grew dusty. But I really

do feel that I did my niche and my practice a disservice by not following up.

Fortunately, I learned my lesson. Now, I focus everything I do
for the benefit of my niche. For example, if I conduct a live seminar,
it's almost always in response to a need of my niche that came to
my attention through my work with them. So I'll record it and make
it available as a free or paid product for my niche. The seminar topic
will generally expand on a previous topic, like expanding an article
to create a book chapter. It might be packaged with other related
programs into a new product, such as a home study program. One
of the great advantages of choosing a niche is that the clients' needs,
questions, and challenges continue to provide me ideas for new products and programs for my service delivery system. I'm always creating new content in efforts to serve them more effectively—it's an
ongoing source of motivation!

CHAPTER SEVEN

Marketing Your Coaching Practice

What *not* to do.

Does marketing create clients?

Marketing versus enrollment.

Basic marketing strategies.

How to market creatively, effectively, and affordably.

So far, I've talked about the importance of marketing and how to usher prospects through the three tiers of your client creation funnel. In this chapter, we go deeper still and look at ways you can market creatively and affordably.

GOOD-BYE, PANELS!

Let's start with this: Most therapists don't think they do *any* marketing at all; but this is often untrue. The hard work—and money—that goes into getting on preferred provider panels is a kind of marketing. After all, the whole point of getting on these panels is to be in a position to enjoy a steady stream of (referred) clients. Of course, many of these same therapists could probably spend less time and effort in building a private-pay practice complete with marketing than they spend dealing with insurance companies, but that often means going outside their comfort zone—something that, regrettably, therapists encourage their clients to do on a daily basis but often neglect in their own professional lives (for the record, I don't think this is hypocrisy; I think it's just an unintentional *vision gap*—the "cobbler's son who has no shoes" kind of thing).

As a coach, you won't have to worry about whether you should care about marketing—because you don't have a choice! Marketing is going to be a routine staple of running your practice. Sure, you'll still benefit from word-of-mouth referrals; but you'll continuously deploy a variety of marketing programs at the same time.

And further, you don't have to stress about marketing, because, believe it or not (and I'm hoping you'll at least give me the benefit of the doubt), marketing can be fun and energizing. Remember, marketing is a way for you to reach out and engage people whom you'd otherwise never meet. What's not fun and energizing about that? And once you've chosen a niche (Chapter 5) and designed your service delivery system for that niche (Chapter 6), you'll find marketing to be a natural extension of your willingness and desire to serve.

WHAT *NOT* TO DO: A TRUE (AND EMBARRASSING) STORY

Before we launch into how to market, it'll be instructive to share with you my personal story of how *not* to do this. It's a bit embarrassing, but I'm willing to subject myself to this dose of humiliation for the greater good of coaching. Ah, the sacrifices. . . .

A few years after starting my private therapy practice, I had a full schedule of managed care clients—but I was being paid half my hourly rate and doing twice the amount of work! And on top of this, I was submitting reports and treatment plans to justify sessions and get more approvals. It was a vicious circle, and even though I was busy, it wasn't the nourishing, sustainable kind of busy.

And as I worked in the middle of this miserable vortex, I knew intuitively that *something* had to change—or more specifically (and harder to admit): *I* had to change something. But what? I desperately wanted to build a private-pay practice working with couples, but had

116

no clue where to begin (or where to stop along the way, or where to end up, for that matter). All I knew was that I needed to *market*. And one day, after feeling the metaphorical water rise up to my neck and threaten to submerge me beneath the dreaded rapids of burnout, I did . . . something different. I opened the local phone book, turned to the yellow pages (this was pre-Internet), and made an appointment with a local so-called marketing consultant.

Now, I'm not going to sit here and write that this marketing consultant was irredeemably incompetent, deceptive, or just plain goofy. Instead, I'll just say that this guy convinced me that direct mail was the route to go. And why not? Apparently, it would allow me to reach thousands of qualified couples in my area for "pennies a lead," and all I needed to do was turn less than 1% of those folks into clients and my dream practice would be full.

However, my gut told me that this wasn't going to work, because, well, we weren't talking about piano lessons or beautiful handcrafted replicas of famous American monuments ("It's suitable for any occasion and makes a great gift, but wait—there's more!"). We were talking *therapy* here. How many people would be open to buying therapy through direct mail? My gut said, "Few, if any," but the rest of me said, "C'mon, David, this guy knows more than you about marketing, and you gotta do something; so do this!" And so I did.

The price tag? $8,000. Yes, that's right: $8,000. That's probably about $12,000 today, maybe more. And to make it even pricier, back then I didn't have $8,000 lying around to spend on marketing. But still, I figured that if $8,000 could fill my practice with the kinds of clients I desperately wanted to help, then it was worth it. And you know what? My friend the marketing consultant agreed with me 100% (what are the odds?).

Of course, you've likely already leaped ahead and know where this story is going. The results? Zero. Zilch. Nothing.

So the final score was marketing consultant: $8,000, David: $0 + humiliation and frustration.

Now, to be accurate and fair, I *did* get calls from a few curious potential clients. But I was flatly unable to do anything with them. I awkwardly responded to questions like "How much do you charge?" "What's your success rate?" "Where did you get your training?" and so on, and not surprisingly, none of these calls turned into clients.

Upon reflection, I realize that my problem was that I didn't know how to enroll them (more on this in Chapter 8); I didn't know how to usher them through the client creation process. I had no clue how to respond in a professional manner that would inspire confidence and result in an appointment.

Okay, let's move into high gear (and away from this sad trip down memory lane) and point at six lessons that I learned from my spectacular marketing failure—lessons that cost me money, time, and effort, but can cost you nothing at all if you'd like to learn from them.

1. You can market till the cows come home and not get any clients. In other words, marketing, by itself, *doesn't* create clients. When it's designed and deployed properly, it plays an important role in the overall picture, but it's not the whole picture itself (regardless of what a smooth-talking marketing consultant promises you!).

2. Spending money is not necessarily effective for solving problems and getting results; in fact, spending (excessive) money can often be counterproductive, because it can mask the real problems and make the symptoms worse.

3. Marketing a private practice is *very* different from marketing other businesses. The folks who sell those quaint replicas of American monuments may, indeed, benefit tremendously from tactics like direct mail marketing. But we as therapists and coaches conduct a very personal, intimate service, and prospective clients must first come to know, like, and trust us before they make the leap and hire us. So the lesson here is: If you don't adjust your marketing plan to embrace the reality of what we do for a living, then that marketing plan is doomed to fail.

4. Marketing consultants don't always know what they're talking about when it comes to *your* unique business. True, some of the principles can be transferable from sector to sector or industry to industry, but just because someone is a dynamo at selling home alarm systems doesn't mean they can sell coaching.

5. Take responsibility for your own marketing solutions. That doesn't mean you shouldn't get help where you need it (such as designing your website, writing your sales material, and so on). But you must be in the driver's seat, at least when things start. As your practice grows, you can start delegating more and more of your marketing to staff or outside help.

6. The following lesson wasn't directly learned through the embarrassing experience I've just shared with you, but it came later and is certainly worth mentioning here while I have your attention: Often, the most effective ways to market and get clients don't cost much at all—sometimes, *nothing* at all. We'll be covering these wonderful low-cost/no-cost marketing ideas in this chapter, so get your highlighter ready.

MARKETING IS COMMUNICATING WHAT YOU DO—NOT CREATING CLIENTS

The primary outcome of marketing, contrary to what I believed long ago, is to create *prospects*, not *clients*. Asking marketing to create clients is, simply, expecting something that it cannot do and is not designed to do. Marketing reaches out into a niche and sparks a relationship; it creates a positive connection. It doesn't make the sale.

Unfortunately, this is a lesson that private-practice professionals (like me) often learn after they've unwisely spent serious money on marketing. They expect their marketing activities to create clients, and spend their efforts on their websites, speaking engagements, writing, and so on; then they are discouraged when they get few—if any—clients as a result.

The other pitfall that I see quite often—particularly among professionals who aren't familiar with marketing—is that they hope the stars will align and clients will emerge from the woodwork. That is, they hope to attract new clients by doing a good job with their existing clients. They take more training, read more books, and work harder for their clients, always hoping that these activities will attract more clients. Alas, they feel helpless and discouraged when their hard work doesn't result in clients flocking to hire them.

So what's the remedy for this sad scenario? Really, it's about accepting the role and limits of marketing and grasping that there is another process that enters the picture, a process that is designed to turn a prospect into a client: *enrollment*.

ENROLLMENT

Enrollment is the process of individually connecting with a prospect with the intention of converting them to a client (when appropriate). That's why a free initial consultation is used by so many professionals: It's the ideal enrollment activity because it gives prospective clients an experience of the professional and increases the likelihood of establishing an ongoing professional relationship.

However, as I've mentioned in previous chapters, I flatly reject the idea of giving away free sessions as part of any marketing strategy (or any other kind of strategy). An initial consultation is just fine, because it gives you and your prospective client a chance to meet, chat, and see if there is mutual benefit in moving forward, which I call the "enrollment conversation." This is far different from actually providing your professional services, which should come only *after* the word *prospective* is done away with, and it's simply you and your paying client.

OF BLUEBIRDS AND BOULDERS

In enrolling clients—that is, moving them from prospect to client—I make a distinction between *bluebirds* and *boulders*.

Bluebirds are those (few, but wonderful) clients who are so strongly attracted to you that they respond to your marketing efforts immediately, fly through your window, and hire you without much of an enrollment process at all. In my experience, most private-practice professionals incorrectly and dangerously expect that life will be full of bluebirds.

Boulders are those (many, but still wonderful) prospects who are interested and attracted to you, yet need to be encouraged—by you—to make the leap from prospect to client.

There's no point in discussing bluebirds, since they're the exception; just be grateful when they come into your life.

Boulders, in contrast, will dominate your enrollment landscape. Truly, it's difficult—even for me, and I've been at this for a while—to understand why some people who appear so interested and eager to move ahead pause and refuse to budge. Usually, the reasons I hear are along the lines of: "Gee, I'd like to, but I just can't afford it right now," or "I don't have the time," or "I'll have to think about it."

Honestly, and I say this with respect to the boulders in my life past, present, and future, I don't think that the hesitation has much to do with time, money, or needing to think about it. Instead, it's plain, old-fashioned fear taking over, and since most people (understandably) won't just come out and say, "David, this coaching thing seems great but I'm kind of freaking out a little and I'm not sure why," they instead find a more digestible rationalization. My response to this is simply to accept that they are experiencing fear, and that my job is to help them overcome it, as appropriate.

My advice in the whole bluebird and boulder universe is simply this: Design your enrollment strategies for the boulders, and the bluebirds will follow.

If the 80/20 rule applies here (and I think it does), you can expect 80% of your clients to be boulders, so if you focus on the bluebirds, you will most likely not have a full practice. The boulders need time to build their relationship with you and trust you enough to take the leap and hire you, which is the purpose of the top and middle activities of the client creation funnel. This is kind of like dating. When you meet someone for the first time, you need a few weeks or months of dates and experiences with them before taking them home and introducing them to your kids or your parents. You start as strangers attracted to each other, and as you get to know one another your boundaries relax, you become increasingly intimate, and before you know it, you're "together."

Two Kinds of Marketing

Although marketing is a science that some people devote their lives to studying, for our purposes we can simplify things and say that there are two kinds of marketing: external and internal.

External marketing is marketing that reaches people you don't know . . . yet! The purpose of external marketing is to create prospects.

With external marketing, you put yourself out there to strangers in your niche, and attract those who resonate with who you are and what you do. Activities that fall under this heading include: advertising; speaking engagements; submitting articles for publication; publishing a book; radio and television appearances; special events such as trade shows, conferences, and festivals; networking events; and Internet marketing venues such as search engines, pay-per-click advertising, and banner exchanges. This is the top of the client creation funnel.

Internal marketing is marketing that builds relationships with your prospects (i.e., people you know and have identified through your client creation funnel), with the goal of having them either hire you or refer you to someone who will.

Sales experts say that 80% of sales require five or more contacts. Internal marketing is how you engage your prospects over time and bring them closer to hiring you. Activities that fall under this heading include: offering complimentary sessions, newsletters and e-zines, e-programs, e-mail broadcasts, mailings, telephone calls, sponsoring a niche community (in-person or online), free or low-cost seminars or events for your subscribers, and a membership system with member benefits. And of course, there is the obvious—and yet rarely applied—internal marketing technique of simply asking people you know for referrals.

PRE-MARKETING REMINDER

Before getting into *how* to market, you must be clear about *who* you're marketing to and *what* you're marketing. Since marketing is communication, it's more effective when targeting a specific audience—which is none other than your niche (which I discussed in Chapter 5). Then you must communicate what you do in a way that makes sense and resonates with these folks. This will focus on your program and service delivery system for them (which I looked at in Chapter 6).

It's also important to note that the primary outcome of marketing is to create *prospects*. I cover how to convert them to clients in Chapter 8. Remember, you can market till the cows come home and not get any clients, so *please* choose a niche, perform your market research, and design your service delivery system before using the strategies outlined in this chapter.

THE FOUNDATION OF MARKETING — CREATING YOUR BRAND

Your brand is the first impression prospective clients experience of you, both in person and otherwise. Your title, business name, program name, website domain name, logo, and mission statement are all parts of your brand. Your brand should be tailored to *both* your specialty and your niche (many people mistakenly focus only on the former). A strong brand is memorable, clear (unambiguous), and attractive to the people you want to reach.

Now, a brand is a *big* thing. In fact, it's less of a thing than it is a name for a bunch of things, like the name of your program, service, website domain name, and practice; the direction that your marketing will point toward; and so on. And because of the *bigness* of brand, it can be daunting and overwhelming to try to create it from scratch, especially if you're just starting out in the brand-building world.

My solution to this is to think small and start with something very easy, practical, and fun: book titles! Here's how it works: As you reflect on what you want to do, ask: "If I were going to write a book for the people in my niche, what would I call it?" Your market research should reveal the top goals, challenges, and needs of the people in your niche, as well as the language (vocabulary, terms, etc.) used to describe these people and their world. Put all of that together, and start thinking of 10 titles of books that you'd write for these people. Here are some examples that should help get your juices flowing.

Hal Runkle (http://www.screamfree.com), a marriage and family therapist, has written *Screamfree Parenting: The Revolutionary Approach to Raising Your Kids by Keeping Your Cool*. This title is *very* effective because it captures Hal's brand and conveys it to the people he wants to reach. And just as effectively, John Van Epp (http://www.nojerks .com) is a former minister who has written *How to Avoid Marrying a Jerk: The Foolproof Way to Follow Your Heart Without Losing Your Mind.* While I'm not crazy about referring to people as jerks, this title is very effective at expressing John's brand and reaching people in his niche—that is, folks who want to avoid negative dating experiences and find their life partner.

Brainstorm and create as many book titles as you can. Ask for help and ideas from friends, family, colleagues, clients, and the people who fit your niche that you identified for your market research. Then, conduct some more market research to see what titles are most preferred by your niche. You may be surprised that your niche favors titles that you wouldn't have put near the top of the list. When this happens, instead of being surprised or even afraid (i.e., you start worrying that you don't really know your niche as well as you thought), be glad and inspired: Your niche is talking to you! Listen to them, and adapt. As I discussed in Chapter 5, your niche *drives* and *determines* what you need to provide. The buck stops with them. So, in other words, don't brand yourself based on what your niche *should* want. Brand yourself based on what they *actually* want. And giving them a list of titles is a very simple, accessible, nontechnical, and fun way for them to share incredibly high-quality information with you.

Another good and easy strategy for identifying the core building blocks of what will ultimately be your brand is to articulate a program name for what your niche wants the *most*. Ask yourself: What powerful words does my niche use to express their desires? For example, if you're working with singles and discover that your niche craves finding their ideal soul mate, then right there you have a potent insight into what may develop into your brand. You may create a program called "How to Find Your Soul Mate," "90 Days to Finding Your Soul Mate," "How to Find Your Soul Mate and Live Happily Ever After," "Finding Your Soul Mate After 50," "The City Girl's Guide to Finding Your Soul Mate," and the list goes on.

All of these exercises are designed to help you find a way *into* your brand. All you need is a small spark to help you clearly see who you are, what you stand for, and what defines you on a professional level. Once you have that in your hand, everything builds from there: your business name, your website domain name, your seminar titles, and so on. All of it will feed back into your brand. It will all be held together by your brand.

And the fun is just starting, because once you've created your brand, you're ready to market!

PRIMARY MARKETING STRATEGY #1: SPEAK YOUR WAY TO MORE CLIENTS

Speaking to groups (aka potential clients) allows you to reach large numbers of people you don't know. These folks are qualified leads because they're interested in your topic. Furthermore, they're interested in *you*; or at least they will be. When you're in front of a group, you're perceived to be the expert, and audiences are inclined to trust you — even before you start talking.

Of course, public speaking doesn't come easily to some (to put it mildly). However, the rewards for overcoming stage fright are enormous and well worth the effort. Here are some tips to help you become a confident, effective public speaker:

o Remember that you *already* talk to people about what you know and do; this is just extending the circle a bit to include people that you want to (and will) know.

o Keep in mind that if you can talk to one person, you can talk to two, three, four, and more people.

o Don't worry if you don't feel that you measure up to some of the great speakers that you know and admire. You don't have to be good to start; you just have to start to be good.

o When all else fails, remember that coaching is your *passion*. And passion alone is the key that allows people to go beyond their comfort zone and into something new, adventurous, exciting, and yes, even daring. You're obviously passionate about being a coach, and furthermore, you're passionate about helping your niche. Tap into these passions to find the motivation you need to overcome your public speaking hurdles.

Although being a good public speaker is helpful, it alone won't create clients for you (unless you have some bluebirds in the audience who are ready to sign up immediately after your standing ovation). To help you usher forward the boulders (small, medium, and large) in your audience, follow these five steps:

1. Create your signature presentation.
2. Practice your presentation.
3. Get speaking engagements.
4. Design your follow-up strategies.
5. Follow up your speaking engagements.

Create Your Signature Presentation

Design a high-quality 45-minute seminar that addresses the biggest goal of the people in your niche (your market research will have told you what this is). Your seminar should be fortified with visuals, handouts, exercises, checklists, and other tools that will wow your audience. You want to do more than inform them—you want to *transform them*, so that they see you as the go-to person for solving a key need.

Practice Your Presentation

To build your confidence and effectiveness, start with groups of people you already know (aka your internal market), including friends and family. Give your signature presentation two or three times to a warm, friendly audience, and request their feedback and suggestions.

Get Speaking Engagements

"Birds of a feather flock together," and there are organized groups for every possible niche. Identify the groups that might be interested in your signature presentation, and begin building a relationship with them, starting as close to the top of the organization's leadership as you can reach. Represent yourself as an allied professional (not as an outsider), and explain that your goals are to learn more about the organization, whom the organization serves, and how you can help the organization serve its members. Don't deviate from this sequence, because if you start with something like, "I'm here to help you do a better job of serving your niche," you'll come across as a salesperson, and that rarely works. If you try to sell organizations on your agenda right away, they'll most likely become leery of you—not because of you personally, but because it's an established fact that people *hate* being sold (however, they quite *enjoy* buying when it's *their* idea!). So again, start by learning more about the organization and its niche. Then roll that information into how you can help the organization do what it wants to do—only in a different and effective way.

Getting in touch with organizational leadership can be a challenge, especially if you try to do it virtually. My recommendation is that you use e-mail and telephone correspondence to set up an in-person meeting.

At that meeting, your goal is to get invited to speak to the organization's membership, preferably at one of its regular meetings (this puts less pressure on you, since the group is meeting anyway). And remember, it's not just the members of the organization who will be evaluating whether there is a solid, ongoing fit; *you* also want to verify that the organization fits with you. Chances are, because you've done your market research long before this, you'll be on the right track. But it's possible that you may discover that things aren't aligned; that is, the group is not receptive to what you're offering. If this happens, look first at the content of your presentation to see if some of the assumptions you made were flawed. For example, your market research may have told you that this niche strongly wants to benefit from the rewards of self-employment, but lacks the confidence, discipline, and vision to get there. Yet in your presentation, you may discover that the biggest challenge they really have is about relationship building, and finding the right people to partner with. In light of this new information, you'll want to adjust your presentation and, by extension, your entire program.

As mentioned, getting yourself noticed and then invited to speak to groups can be a challenge. If you find the attempt frustrating, consider hosting your own speaking engagements. You do this simply by setting a time, date, and place, and marketing your event to your niche (both internally and externally). If bringing everyone together in the same room is a logistical hassle or financially burdensome, then consider teleclasses and teleseminars conducted via conference calls. These are cost-effective, and allow you to reach people who couldn't or wouldn't attend your in-person event. To leverage your marketing I recommend conducting teleseminars in addition to your in-person seminars to cast a wider net and reach more people with the same marketing activities.

Design Your Follow-Up Strategies

Strategize ways to follow up with your niche. Start by planning for three distinct groups:

1. Strongly attracted prospects who see you as the answer to their prayers and are ready to hire you (aka bluebirds)
2. Moderately attracted prospects who are ready for a small step, such as buying your book (aka small boulders)
3. Mildly attracted prospects who are interested, but not ready to commit money (aka medium-sized boulders)

You'll note that we aren't even going to bother with big boulders. Frankly, they're probably not even in the audience, though some may get dragged there by a friend or significant other. Every now and then, a big boulder becomes a smaller boulder, and that's great to see. These folks tend to be super-friendly, and somewhat amazed—even in shock—at how much sense you make. And then there are big boulders who remain big boulders. They sit with their arms crossed and glare the whole time (usually at the person who dragged them there). Ignore them and don't feel bad that they aren't moving forward. It's not your fault. Remember: You aren't in the business of reshaping boulders. You're in the business of serving your niche. Leave the task of reshaping to others; it's not your role, or your responsibility.

Let's go back to the three groups who matter. You want to offer each of these groups something special that will encourage them to move forward. You have several options. You can offer a big discount for folks who sign up for your workshop on the spot, a reasonably priced (or specially discounted) book or home study program, and a free audio CD for everyone who signs up for your mailing list. Weave these options into your presentation, handouts, and follow-up; don't deliver them as a list all at once!

Then, plan your post-seminar follow-up strategies and build your relationship with participants (internal marketing) that eventually leads them to hire you and/or refer others to you (more about this in Chapter 8).

Follow Up Your Speaking Engagements

Implement your follow-up strategies (see Chapter 8) and build your relationship with the participants who have joined your mailing list, purchased your home study program, and so on. Offer them a free strategy session (e.g., "How to Find Your Soul Mate Strategy Session") as a bonus in appreciation for joining your mailing list (see Chapter 8 for specific instructions about how to conduct strategy sessions). Invite them to your next seminar. Send them a bonus report, article, tip sheet, and so on. Send them a discount coupon for your next workshop. For free strategy sessions or discounts, be sure to provide an expiration date to encourage them to act quickly. And don't forget to ask for their referrals! For example, "Please pass this along to your interested friends or family members," or "Please forward this to someone you know who would benefit from this information," or in some situations, "Please pass this along to singles you care about."

Tip: Be sure to record your speaking engagements to create products such as downloadable audio programs, audio CDs, home study programs, and the like.

PRIMARY MARKETING STRATEGY #2: WRITE YOUR WAY TO MORE CLIENTS

Writing is a potent and cost-effective way to share your expertise and information with your niche. Writing enables you to:

- Attract prospects (external marketing).
- Build relationships and provide value to your network (internal marketing).
- Create products for passive income and multiple revenue streams.

Here are some low-cost, practical, and (relatively) easy ways to market your coaching practice with writing.

Write Articles

As part of your market research, make a list of your niche's top problems and questions. Then make a list of the strategies and steps needed to resolve those problems and answer those questions. Every item on your list has the potential to be a great article. So say good-bye to not knowing what to write about!

I'm commonly asked whether a shorter article is better, or a longer one. The answer is somewhere in the middle at about 500 to 700 words. Anything shorter than this typically can't do justice to a topic. Anything longer may be full of useful information, but won't be read due to its length. If you have a topic that demands more than 700 words, simply break it up into smaller pieces, and name each article "Part 1," "Part 2," and so on. In fact, this *series* strategy can make for some very compelling reading, since folks who read earlier articles in the series will be that much more inclined to read later ones.

As you work with your clients and communicate with the people in your niche, continuously capture the questions and problems that come to your attention, and add them to your list of article topics. The feedback you get from existing articles can also be full of ideas and pointers on what to write about next.

Publish Your Articles

We live in a glorious era of self-publishing, and that means you can and should publish all of your content (articles, newsletters, etc.) on both your coaching website and your social networking websites (e.g., Facebook, Twitter, etc.). This content not only adds depth and value to your website, but it also tells search engines that your website is full of good stuff, which is one of the criteria that Google and the others look for when they rank websites (it's not the only criterion, but it's a big one).

Speaking of doing things that Google likes, you can also publish your articles in one or several of the many article directories on the Internet. These directories are free and have five main benefits for you:

1. Your articles will show up in search engine results when people look for related information.
2. Folks who want to learn about a particular topic find and browse article directories and search by category and topic.
3. You could find some great potential clients this way because people often visit article directories the same way they visit (or used to visit) libraries.
4. Websites, blogs, e-zines, and other online and offline publishers that need related content can find and republish your article (provided that your contact information and author credit remain unchanged).
5. Your articles will include a resource box at the bottom with a short bio and link to your website, which will do two things for you: encourage readers to visit your website for more information, and increase your search engine ranking.

Each time your article is published on the Internet (on a website somewhere . . . *anywhere*), Google and the other search engines say: "Hey, this coaching website is valuable and the kind of site we want to encourage searchers to visit, because there is a link pointing to it." Obviously, one article linking back to your coaching website isn't going to persuade Google that you rule the coaching universe. But if there are several, the impact is cumulative.

Let me add a few additional remarks about article directories, because it's an interesting concept.

o Submitting your articles individually to numerous article directories can be time consuming. I use and recommend using an online article syndication or submission service that (once set up) automatically syndicates or distributes your articles to dozens, even hundreds of related article directories, blogs, and so on.

o Your articles (the ones you publish on your own site, and those that you publish in article directories) should be optimized for specific keywords. It's beyond the scope of this book to explain keywords in detail and how to optimize your articles for them. Besides, if you want to learn about this subject, there is plenty of free advice on the Web. For now, it's just something that I wanted to mention here because if I neglected to do so and you had some keyword experience (or just heard one of your kids mumbling about it while typing away on a BlackBerry), then you might start to worry a little. Again, do some research or connect with an experienced search marketing consultant.

Information Products

Your articles and other content can, in time, be compiled into tip sheets, special reports, e-courses, booklets, manuals, workbooks, home study programs, and even full-fledged books. Yes, you read that correctly! The idea of writing a book may be daunting, but if you have 50 articles on a topic you can create a book simply by putting all of them together. You can then distribute it as an e-book, or even self-publish it and print out hard copies, which you then sell or give away at your workshops, seminars, and so on.

Media

The Internet has transformed press release distribution because there are so many websites and media sources out there that need content, and there has never been so much specialization. Do you love red M&M's? There's probably a website (maybe more than one) devoted to this. Think that a certain breed of dog is therapeutic? Chances are you aren't alone and there's a niche out there that cares as much as—maybe more than—you do. My point is that whereas in the old days news had to be really big in order to be picked up by old-school media (such as newspapers and television stations), these days the field is wide open, which means you should be writing and distributing press releases on a regular basis.

There are both paid and free ways to distribute your press releases. As you can imagine, the paid routes are considered more credible by more established media sources; however, there is no guarantee that even if you pay to have your press release distributed it will get picked up by major media. This is, indeed, a crushing realization for some people who spend hundreds of dollars on a press release and discover, to their shock, that the *New York Times* and CNN simply don't care, and Oprah isn't calling. But then again, all it takes is a nibble from any major source and your press release could become a business gift that keeps on giving.

The free press release distribution route is a bit more flexible. Your press release *will* spread around the Internet, but may never even be seen by (so-called) credible media sources. This may not be such a bad thing; again, all you need are a few nibbles in the right places and your press release will generate lots of positive attention for you.

Whichever route you choose—paid or free—just remember these basic press release principles:

o Your press release must be *newsworthy*, not promotional. Yes, okay, it's newsworthy to you that you opened a new coaching practice. But is that really news with a capital *N*? No, I'm afraid not. However, the fact that you're "a new coach and serving [enter your niche here] through [enter the ways you serve here]" *is* newsworthy. If you target a specific publication (and some outlets will let you submit a press release to them directly from their websites), you position your press release to succeed and be loved if you really get a handle on the media outlet's audience. For example, if you submit a press release to *Working Mother* magazine, then your press release should target that specific audience. Often, media outlets will give you some tips on what their audience is looking for. Other times, you'll have to do some digging. Really, it only takes a few minutes of your time to get a handle on whom you're writing for. Keep in mind that media outlets *want you to make their jobs easier*—and if you can supply them with valuable content for their audience, they'll likely pick up on your press release. They aren't doing it for you; they're doing it for them. But hey, that's okay. Everyone wins.

On top of press releases, you may also consider "Letters to the Editor" as a strategy for getting some good media publicity. Sometimes, reporters may even contact you to follow up, provided that you put enough identifying information in the letter itself.

PRIMARY MARKETING STRATEGY #3: NETWORK YOUR WAY TO MORE CLIENTS BY BUILDING YOUR REFERRAL SYSTEM

It is well documented that by far the most effective way that private-practice professionals get clients is word-of-mouth referrals. And so besides being basic and traditional, this is also the single most productive way to get clients and build your practice. Here's how to get started:

Referrals can come from anyone: friends and family, clients and former clients. This last group, in particular, can be the most helpful because they've benefited from working with you, and would actually appreciate a way to give back to you by referring others.

I recommend you organize your potential referral sources into six referral pipelines:

Referral pipeline #1: Current and former clients. Maintain your current and former client contact information in an organized and easily accessible database for all your referral activities.

Referral pipeline #2: Prospects (whom you know). These are people who already know you, such as friends and family members, people who have inquired about your services but have not yet enrolled, and people you know but haven't contacted in a while.

Referral pipeline #3: New contacts (whom you don't know). You'll be meeting new people all the time, and each of those contacts will be added to your pipeline. Just remember to enter these into your database on a regular basis so those business cards and slips of paper help you build your business instead of piling up in a drawer.

Referral pipeline #4: Colleagues. Just as with your current and former clients, create and maintain contact information for your colleagues in an organized and easily accessible database for all referral activities.

Referral pipeline #5: Complementary professionals. Ask yourself: "What other needs do my clients have?" Identify the professionals and service providers who, like you, connect with your niche, and build referral relationships with them.

Referral pipeline #6: Organizations. As mentioned earlier, birds of a feather flock together, and there are groups and organizations for every possible niche. These organizations include professional associations, chambers of commerce, local chapters of national organizations, welcome wagons, schools, churches, university clubs, and more.

You should plan to contact at least one new referral source per week, though early in your practice you may need to contact more. And speaking of contacting referral sources: Are you one of those people who don't like (okay, *hate*) asking for referrals? Are you worried that it might seem like you're imposing on people to ask them for leads? If so, while that sentiment is understandable, it's typically misplaced. The majority of people you want to ask for referrals in the first place—that is, people you like, and who like you—*want* to see you succeed as a coach. They won't balk at trying to help you if they can. And organizations have a clear self-interest in referring you to their members, simply because part of their mandate is to provide value and be of help to their members. So if your coaching services fit into that category, they'll gladly agree to refer potential clients to you (just as you would if you were in their shoes).

Also, make it easy for people to refer others to you by providing collateral materials (such as a cover letter, brochure, tip sheet, references, CD or DVD, gift certificate for your free strategy session, etc.) assembled into a folder or envelope, which they can send or give to the people they wish to refer to you. Other ways to make it easy for your referrals to reach you include providing prestamped and preaddressed envelopes, a designated telephone line or voice mail box with an outgoing message especially for prospective clients, or even a special Web page designed just for referred clients (these small websites are often called "microsites" or "landing pages").

CREATIVE MARKETING STRATEGIES

Once you've mastered the primary marketing strategies, you can expand upon them with these creative alternatives:

"Tupperware Parties"

Do you remember Tupperware parties? They were built on the premise that inviting folks into your home and offering them quality information (and, yes, Tupperware) was a positive marketing experience that both presenters and guests enjoyed (the Jell-O mold, however, is another story).

You can apply Tupperware thinking to your marketing strategies. This is one of my favorite creative marketing strategies, and by itself might be all you need to fill your practice.

You can either host the gathering yourself or ask someone you know (e.g., a friend, colleague, client, referral source, etc.) to host a gathering of their network for a private seminar. It can take place in a home or an office.

This can be a fun, intimate gathering of like-minded friends and acquaintances who are highly qualified prospects for you (remember: birds of a feather flock together!).

Joint Ventures

Contact the professionals and organizations in your referral pipelines (pipelines #5 and #6) and invite them to discuss the mutual benefits of collaboration. You have your resources and platforms, they have their resources and platforms, and collectively you can reach more people, provide more value, and create more clients than any of you could on your own.

Joint ventures typically work in one of two ways. You can co-conduct and co-market an event. Or, you can promote complementary professionals and organizations to your network, and they can promote you to theirs. This latter approach is probably where you'll start, since it's quick, easy, low-cost (in fact, *no*-cost), and effective. However, the more closely you work with a partner in your pipeline, the more you may want to do something together, which could be incredibly valuable in the long term.

Contests

Contests are a great way to generate some positive buzz while introducing prospects to your coaching practice. Start by having a contest for the people in your niche (you can branch out as your practice grows, but for now, stick to your specialty).

In my world, I conduct a "Conscious Dating® Success Story of the Year" contest each year around Valentine's Day. The stories I receive are inspirational and instructive, and in a way they're testimonials for my program—which helps sell my books, plus it convinces prospects that, yes, conscious dating really works! The winners get a valuable prize (like an iPod), and their story is published on my website and publicized in my Conscious Dating newsletter, blog, and Twitter feed, and through press releases.

Giveaways

Giveaways, like contests, are a great way to generate publicity and, at the same time, develop and deepen your relationship with your niche (which, as I've mentioned before and will mention again, is *the* most important relationship in your practice). Your giveaway can involve a product, service, or both. It can also be time-limited, so create some urgency (otherwise, your prospects may avoid taking action because they assume they can get the freebies anytime).

In my practice, around mid-December each year, I invite my Conscious Dating newsletter subscribers to order a free copy of my book to give to a friend or family member over the holiday season (they only have to pay for shipping and handling). Just like the contest example I mentioned, the giveaway helps promote the book and my programs for singles.

Scholarships and Pro Bono Services

As a coach, you'll encounter people who want to enroll in your program but claim that they can't afford it. As a therapist, you may be inclined to offer a discount (a "sliding scale"). I strongly advise you not to do this; instead, I recommend that you create a limited number of scholarships and advertise them. This will help your community, and ensure that the people who receive your discounted rates indeed qualify for them (as opposed to people who don't mind spending money on a house or car they can't afford, but want *you* to lower *your* rates).

If you create some scholarship opportunities, I advise following these guidelines:

- Have a predetermined number of scholarships—no more than two pro bono individual clients.
- Offer a limited duration, such as 60 to 90 days of coaching; otherwise you can create the expectation that you'll provide months, even *years* of free service.
- Make your scholarship available to new clients only; you don't want previous clients using this to receive continued or new free services.
- Ask your scholarship recipients to provide you with a referral and a testimonial if they're satisfied with your services.
- Put all of these guidelines in writing.

An added benefit to scholarships is that you'll typically generate a waiting list for your services. This will allow you to honestly and directly tell any prospect who wants free services: "Yes, I do accept a limited number of pro bono clients in my practice, but I currently have a six-month waiting list. Would you like an application for one of my pro bono slots, or would you prefer to get started right away?" You'll be amazed at how many prospects will magically find the money, rather than wait six months!

Sponsors

It may happen that your niche is composed of people who typically have limited financial means relative to other niches. For example, you may want to reach out and help college students, high school athletes, teenage unwed mothers, homeless veterans, and so on.

To help these people take advantage of your coaching, try to help them identify people in their lives (friends, family members, etc.) who might provide them with some financial help, either in whole or in part. In my experience, if these people are truly motivated to work with you, they'll either find the money to avoid asking for help or they'll lean on their support system (which can actually be very helpful as part of their growth).

And in your marketing, you can target the people who have a vested interest in helping your niche receive coaching (e.g., parents of college-bound high school seniors, etc.).

Free Starter Programs

Multi-session programs require higher commitment than a free session. As we all know, people are much more willing to sign up for a free program instead of a paid one. So with that in mind, a free starter program can be a potent marketing strategy. Once your clients have experienced value and momentum by completing the beginning steps, they'll be more likely to sign up to continue and get all of the benefits and results of your program.

Teleseminars

Conducting speaking engagements by telephone can be even more effective than in-person events for these reasons:

- Participants are more likely to fit you into their schedule if they don't have to travel.
- Low-cost (or *no*-cost!) overhead means that your event can be offered for free.
- You can potentially reach more people since your audience can join you from anywhere in the world.
- There's a low barrier to entry, because you don't need any infrastructure.
- Your teleseminars allow you to create immediate products; many conference call services allow you to record the event, which becomes an instant audio product.

If you're unfamiliar with the ins and outs of teleseminars, attend as many different ones as you can find, and pay attention to how others are structuring and managing the events. Also take note of their marketing strategies and their follow-up methods. Some of the things you learn will impress you; some will not. Take the good stuff and build your teleseminar around that. Oh, and before you launch yourself out there, you may want to conduct your first teleseminars for the people in your network, just to increase your comfort level.

Teleclinics

Teleclinics are conference calls designed in a question-and-answer format (similar to a call-in radio show). Teleclinics are a great marketing activity, because everyone who participates is identifying himself or herself as a potential client. Your interaction with them is an audition for what it's like to work with you. With practice, teleclinics can be a lot of fun (who wouldn't want to play "Dr. Laura" or "Dr. Phil"?), can provide a lot of value, and can help you create a lot of clients. Be sure to follow up with participants, and let them know that their problems simply cannot be solved in a 5- to 10-minute conversation.

And as a bonus, teleclinics can give you great ideas for articles, seminars, and products for your niche.

Niche Communities

We covered niche communities in Chapter 5 (so head on back there if you need to!).

Live Events

Live events include socials, seminars, workshops and classes, networking, fund-raisers, and other significant gatherings. Live events can be tricky, and while I'm noting them here as a marketing strategy, I'm advising that you put them on hold until your practice starts to take flight. This is because live events can require considerable up-front costs to produce (both materials and support staff), and if there are any key design weaknesses, they can fail—and put a serious dent in your budget, not to mention your enthusiasm. With that having been said, live events are a powerful way to reach large groups, generate significant sales of your products and programs, and create large numbers of clients at one time. For example, I filled my new coaching practice in 90 days after launching my weekly Friday Night Social for singles.

Workshops and Classes

As we discussed in Chapter 6, workshops and classes are valuable features of your service delivery system, and very effective ways to attract large numbers of potential clients. Many graduates will join your group coaching program, or they'll hire you for individual coaching to support what they've learned in your workshops and classes.

Fund-Raisers

Schools, churches, and nonprofits are always seeking ways to raise funds, and will most likely be open to your proposal if it fits their values and missions. You can donate a percentage of your product and service sales to a worthy cause, or host a live event and donate the proceeds. Fund-raisers are great for joint ventures and can allow you to partner with schools, churches, and nonprofits, giving you access to their networks. Just remember that whatever cause you identify must resonate with your niche. Your market research will help you choose the right fund-raising partner and approach.

Public Service Campaigns

You're in the business of helping people, so it is not hard to identify a public service angle for your specialty and niche. For example, after reading headline after headline about the high unemployment rate during a recent recession, I put together a seminar on "Secrets of Self-Employment," and focused on tips for starting a small business. Furthermore, once you've designed a public service campaign related to your practice, it's easy to get joint venture partners and media coverage for your worthy cause.

Sponsorships

Corporations seeking to fulfill their community support missions (or just wanting the good publicity that comes with being seen as a caring, helpful community partner) are typically open to creative ways that will promote their brand and enhance their image with their potential customers. While getting your foot in the door by yourself might be a challenge, if you have nonprofit partners (see the next strategy), this can give you the clout and connections you need to make things happen.

Nonprofit Partnerships

Nonprofit organizations, including churches, schools, public service agencies, and other nongovernmental organizations (NGOs), are always seeking ways to raise funds and are open to fund-raising partnerships. In addition, they're always seeking ways to stretch their resources, provide their services more effectively, and serve their constituencies—especially if it doesn't cost them anything!

When pitching your ideas to nonprofits, remember to ensure that they understand the value to their congregation, membership, or audience. For example, churches and schools will typically *not* let you sell or market to their group, but if you provide a genuine service — say, relationship coaching to married couples, or nutrition and wellness advice to college-bound students — then you can position yourself to be a highly valued information resource.

Ask Campaigns

An ask campaign is both a market research and a marketing activity. For your market research, ask as many people as you can a question, such as: "What is your most important question about finding your life partner?" (Obviously, you'd ask about whatever is a top priority for your niche; I'm using an example from my world.) The responses will generate a gold mine of ideas for your articles, seminars, programs, and so forth. This can be a particularly effective marketing strategy when hosted on your website. Set up an autoresponder and invite participants to opt in to join your seminar, participate in a conference call, or get a special report (or whatever else you're offering) for them to find the answer.

LEVERAGING TECHNOLOGY/INTERNET MARKETING

Today's world is very different for private-practice professionals compared to the old days of spending hundreds or thousands of dollars on yellow pages ads, or relying on insurance referrals and reimbursements. Now, you can reach the world from your computer and attract the kinds of clients you want to help using ways that were unimaginable just a decade ago. By effectively leveraging technology and Internet marketing, you enable yourself to help more people, make a much bigger difference, and generate *far* more income than you may have thought possible when you started training as a therapist.

Telephone

Although the telephone has been around for a long time, conference calling services and Internet telephony (Skype, Vonage, Magic Jack, etc.) now allow us to effectively and economically market to

143

and serve a worldwide audience. The telephone has enabled me to transition from a traditional private practice to working full time from home touching the lives of hundreds of thousands (perhaps millions) of singles and couples all over the world in the past 13 years with my books, websites, online and telephone programs, and so forth. Be sure to get a comfortable headset!

Website

Your website must not simply be an online brochure for your practice. It should be designed to attract and interact with your niche and deliver valuable information and resources through opt-in offers such as a downloadable audio program, video, special report, and so on. You can use your website to sell your products and to generate passive income by promoting the products and programs of others (just ensure that they're valuable to your niche and won't compete with what you offer). You can also create a niche community (see Chapter 5) by hosting a forum or membership system on your website.

Also make sure that your website is easy to find, both by search engines (through the use of keywords and quality backlinks) and by members of the media, who may want to interview you. Make sure your contact information is easily found and up to date. While your website should be designed to provide value to your niche (and not be all about you), be sure your photo and bio are easy to find for those who want to know more about you.

Search Engine Optimization (SEO)

Search engines index Web page content through keywords that appear in the headers, body text, links, graphics, and so on, to show relevant results for Internet searches. Your goal is to find the keywords most used by your niche to find information and resources related to your specialty, and optimize your website to appear high in the search results for those keywords. You can pay for top ranking via pay-per-click advertising, but organic searches are often preferred because there is no cost involved; it's basically free advertising.

Again, there's plenty of information about how to do this that is freely available on the Internet, and it may be worth your while to hire an expert to help you.

Autoresponder

You're no doubt familiar with a vacation autoresponder, which is the mechanism that sends you a reply when the person you just tried to e-mail is away on vacation. In marketing terms, an autoresponder is similar and also different.

It's similar in that it's automated; that is, you don't have to manually do anything. A prospect enters his or her e-mail address, clicks "submit" (or whatever the button might say), and automatically starts receiving messages from you.

The different part is that a marketing autoresponder is a *series* of messages, usually called a "serial" or "sequential" autoresponder (whereas the "vacation" version is just one message). The reason it's a series is simply because you can't convey the totality of your message in just one response, and multiple contacts build your relationship and enhance your marketing and enrollment. For example, you may have created an autoresponder outlining the "10 Biggest Reasons Why Relationships Fail," and each reason may need 200 to 300 words. To send people a 2,000- to 3,000-word e-mail is just not feasible; their eyes will glaze over and they'll hit the "trash" button. But if you break it up, you can deliver your message in nice, small, bite-sized chunks. Furthermore, in each message you include a call to action, which invites prospects to visit your website and do something (e.g., sign up for a program or purchase a book at a discount). Or perhaps you'll even encourage them to pick up the phone and call you for a consultation. You can have more than one call to action per message—though you really shouldn't have more than two or three (or else it just sounds like a sales effort).

Once someone subscribes to your autoresponder, they're giving you permission to send them information. However, you *must* include an easy and clear way for them to unsubscribe (this is typically found at the very end of the autoresponder, in the footer of the message). Some people even prefer using what's called "double opt-in" autoresponders. These strangely dubbed beasts require subscribers to confirm that, yes, they are the ones who signed up for your autoresponder in the first place. This prevents spam and people from signing up others without their knowledge.

Here are some ways you can use an autoresponder:

- Deliver an e-program or e-course through installments.
- Send out an e-zine (a digital/Web-based newsletter or magazine).
- Provide a link to a special report, audio, or video program (you can also offer this as the *incentive* for people to subscribe to your autoresponder in the first place).
- Use it to conduct sales follow-ups.
- Use it to announce events.
- Broadcast your follow-up messages, announcements, and offers as needed (not all messages need to be preprogrammed—you can send a message to your subscribers anytime you like).

Blog

While a website is static (it doesn't change much from day to day), your blog is dynamic and the ideal place to post your articles, announcements, Q&A responses, musings, and more. The purpose of your blog is to constantly and consistently offer valuable content to your niche. As a bonus, search engines seek out and index new content, and the more productive and popular your blog is, the more traffic it will generate—which means more prospects at no cost!

E-Zine

Electronic newsletters—called e-zines—are a great, cost-effective way to stay in touch with your niche. Design your e-newsletter or e-zine content around what your niche will find valuable, such as tips, book reviews, "Ask the Coach" sections, articles, lists, and so on. Yes, you can have some promotional material in here as well, but make sure that you don't reduce your newsletter to little more than a commercial. Remember: If it's not seen as valuable and helpful by your niche members, they'll reject it the same way that *you* would if you were in their shoes.

If you wish, you can also print out your newsletter and have it in your office, or bring it to your workshops and so on. However, due to cost concerns, plus the fact that e-newsletters are much more versatile than print newsletters because they can have links to websites and other media (video, audio, etc.), e-newsletters are much more practical. However, ensure that your niche determines this — not you. For example, if you're serving seniors who want to live as independently as possible, sending them e-newsletters may assume a technical sophistication and comfort that they don't have — which means they won't get the e-newsletter in the first place, or they won't read it when they do. In most cases, your niche will be savvy enough to benefit from an e-newsletter, but not always. Do your market research (are you tired of reading that yet?).

Your autoresponder system can manage your e-zine easily and cost effectively so that you can focus on generating new content instead of managing lists and subscribers. Furthermore, you can send other follow-up messages to subscribers, such as bonus information or marketing messages. Just make sure that you have their permission, and consider a double opt-in system to confirm that you're reaching people who want your stuff.

Social Networking

Social networking is a potent business and marketing tool, and you should use these services to engage your niche. When used effectively, Twitter, Facebook, and other social networking websites allow you to reach millions of potential clients. You can create a Twitter feed specifically for your niche and link to your other social networking accounts so that your updates automatically get published on Facebook and elsewhere. I have a Twitter feed for singles (http://twitter .com/findmysoulmate), couples (http://twitter.com/consciouslove), and practice building (http://twitter.com/fullpractice). They all allow me to easily, quickly, and at no cost (other than a few minutes of my time) reach my three most important niches.

Pay-per-Click Advertising

Pay-per-click advertising is an innovative, Web-driven concept that lets you advertise and pay *only* when a lead clicks on your ad. To be effective, your pay-per-click campaign must integrate with your website so that when prospects click a link and go immediately to your site (or to an intermediary site, sometimes called a "splash page" or "landing page"), they are easily ushered through your sales funnel and encouraged to take a desired action—such as signing up for your e-zine, downloading a free report, making an appointment with you, or some other clear, progressive action that changes them from mere interested visitors into qualified leads. Keep in mind that an ineffective pay-per-click campaign can waste *a lot* of money, just as I did with direct mail so many years ago. Designing and testing effective ads, researching and bidding on effective keywords, tracking return on investment (ROI), and converting visitors to customers and clients are all crucial to effective pay-per-click advertising campaigns, and frankly, it's beyond the knowledge and skills of most therapists and coaches. Therefore, I recommend outsourcing this function to an expert. If you have the budget for advertising, this can be your most effective (and cost-effective) alternative.

Link and Banner Exchange

This is the online version of word-of-mouth referral. You can have an area of your website for "Resources" where you feature the links and banners of products and services you recommend (some or all might have affiliate programs that generate a commission if a sale is made, providing you passive income), and other websites reciprocate by linking to your website or hosting your banners.

Just remember that all of the links and banners on your website must be relevant to your niche and fit the theme of your practice. Similarly, the websites that link to you must be relevant to your niche, which will bring you qualified traffic and enhance your search engine ranking.

Affiliate Program

Affiliate programs allow you to track online referrals and to compensate affiliates who refer future clients and customers to you. A well-designed affiliate campaign recruits and trains affiliates, and provides them with the tools they need to be successful (e.g., banners, links, sales letters, e-mail messages, tweets, etc.). Once it's established, your affiliate program can continue indefinitely, and be applied to new products and programs as you launch them. In fact, affiliate programs are so popular and rewarding when done right that many blog and website owners make it their full-time business!

Shopping Cart

Though not marketing tools themselves some shopping carts are integrated solutions for online businesses that include autoresponders and affiliate programs as well as the ability to put your products, programs, and services on your website and accept online payments. Most private-practice professionals don't have products and programs and therefore don't need a shopping cart. As you build your coaching practice and add products and programs for your niche(s), though, a shopping cart allows you to effectively manage your online transactions.

Portal

Portals are websites that aggregate content for a particular audience, and are great places for you to submit articles and other relevant content (different portals have their own rules as to what can and cannot be submitted for publication). For example, the Relationship Coaching Institute provides the content and experts for the relationship section of Boomer-Living.com.

A Final Word on Marketing

Marketing is a huge topic that has been the subject of entire books. My intent with this chapter is to introduce you to what marketing is, give you solid information to help you get started, provide you creative and fun alternatives for marketing, and introduce you to the tools of marketing online. My best advice is to start with the three primary forms of marketing—speaking, writing, and networking— and build from there. Don't spend a lot of money until your coaching practice is generating income and you know that your money will be well spent. Remember that the most effective ways to market are free or low-cost, and please keep in mind my $8,000 direct mail disaster! Also, don't be tempted to save money by learning how to build your own website, do your own pay-per-click advertising campaign, or set up your own blog, shopping cart, or affiliate program. Your time is much better spent on the primary forms of marketing, enrollment, and working with your clients, which will provide you the income to pay others to do the tasks that it doesn't pay for you to do; and being experts, they can perform those tasks more professionally and more effectively than you can. Now it's time to focus on enroll- ment strategies to help you convert prospects to clients, which is the key to private-practice success as a coach or private-pay therapist.

CHAPTER EIGHT

How to Enroll Clients for Your Coaching Practice

How getting coaching clients differs from getting therapy clients.
Selling versus enrollment.
Conducting an effective enrollment conversation.
How to get a client whenever you want.

Getting quality clients for your coaching practice is *very* different from doing the same for your therapy practice.

For starters, as covered in Chapter 2, coaching clients are functional people who hire you to help them get results and achieve goals. Therapy clients are typically dysfunctional people who hire you—or more technically, have their insurance company hire you on their behalf—to solve their problems and ease their emotional and psychological pain. (This brings up a side point. A prospective client may want to try to use their insurance benefits to pay for your coaching. In a word: *Don't.*)

The difference between coaching and therapy clients is also a matter of enrollment. As mentioned in Chapter 7, getting clients (enrollment) is a *huge* topic and deservedly so. In this chapter we focus on understanding the nuances of enrollment, and practical, effective strategies you can start using immediately.

As a therapist, you're contacted by many folks who self-identify their need for therapy. And even if they aren't thrilled about the idea of therapy, they aren't antagonistic to it; that is, they are, at least at the beginning, going along with the program. Calling such clients "self-motivated" paints the wrong picture because they're motivated more by pain, but it's fair enough to say that they're "self-directed."

As a coach, life isn't so simple. There are precious few ready-made clients who wake up one day and say to themselves: *Wow, you know what? I need coaching!* Sure, it *can* happen, and with the increasing emergence of coaching as a legitimate helping profession—complete with things like certification, quality training, continuing education requirements, and, hey, even books like this one (if I do say so myself)—it's even predictable. But for now, there aren't going to be many folks who knock on your door without any external nudge.

That external nudge, fortunately, can and will come from many sources. One of them will be word-of-mouth marketing—your satisfied clients will create prospective clients. Another way will be through professional referrals from other therapists and helping professionals. And then, of course, there's your marketing! That's the nudge that we're focusing on here.

Now, as you've (I hope) come to realize already (unless you skipped straight from the Preface to this chapter—that's okay!), creating marketing systems, strategies, and services that work isn't agonizingly hard. In fact, compared to the rigorous training that you experienced just to become a licensed therapist, it's a cakewalk. But I'd mislead you if I implied that effective marketing just happens by itself. It *does* take some work. However, the rewards can be immense and lasting.

Remember: As challenging as your marketing commitment may be (and it won't be *that* challenging), it's far more challenging to get paid less than you want, to help fewer clients than you want, and to generally just *do* less than you want with your professional life. Indeed, as I often told my kids (or rather, told their rolling eyeballs) when I wanted them to understand that spending the time and effort to study and get their homework done correctly the first time is far easier than taking shortcuts and having to redo assignments: "In life, sometimes the long way is the short way, and the short way is the long way." Applied to the marketing tasks ahead of you, while you can resist and avoid doing them because they fall outside of your comfort zone, you'll simply be short-circuiting your success. In other words (although it may seem bizarre for a therapist like you who might have succeeded professionally so far *without* relying on marketing), the shortest and best way to get to where you want to be from where you are now is by learning and applying solid marketing and enrollment skills.

The remainder of this chapter focuses on introducing you to some solid enrollment strategies and skills so that you can build a lucrative and fulfilling coaching practice. And remember—especially for those who've skipped to this chapter—*you do not have to give up your therapy practice in order to build a thriving coaching practice!* In fact, the marketing and enrollment skills you learn and apply to your coaching will, in ways that you probably can't see right now, profoundly improve your therapy practice because they'll help you work with the clients you want to help, and generate the income you desire.

SELLING VERSUS ENROLLMENT

Many helping professionals resist marketing and enrollment because it feels like selling, which they believe is contrary to their values. In my view, *selling* is attempting to influence someone to purchase a product or service, while *enrollment* is building a relationship with someone to see if your services are a good fit for that person. Enrollment, then, involves getting to know people, appreciating their needs, establishing trust, and then offering a solution that *they* can decide to buy—or not to buy. In this light, enrollment is not about selling lemon used cars to little old ladies. It's about creating a dialogue with people whom you'd never be able to reach without marketing.

So put it all together, and it says: If you have a stigma associated with marketing, then it's in your interest to get rid of it—or at least suspend it—until you can get your feet wet in marketing, and see that when it's created properly, it can be as authentic and have as much integrity as you do.

ENROLLMENT PREREQUISITES

Now, I can safely assume that if you talk to enough people, you'll eventually land a client. However, this "shotgun" approach is impractical, which means that in order to build a successful coaching practice, you must increase your client conversion rate from "once in a while" to "most of my qualified prospects." The following pointers help you do this.

Qualify Your Prospects

Your prospects must be qualified; that is, they must fit your target audience, be motivated to change, be committed to results, understand the value of your services, and appreciate the need to make a significant financial investment to get their desired outcome. I'll state it bluntly: Your enrollment efforts will be wasted on unqualified prospects, so don't bother.

Anticipate Their Core Questions About Trust and Credibility

You also need to anticipate and address the needs of your prospective clients so that you can clearly and authentically answer questions like: "Can I trust you?" and "What qualifies you to do this?" Your prospects likely won't ask you these questions; instead, they'll just think them. That's why you need to anticipate and proactively provide the answers. And to drill even further, in order to provide those answers, you need to be able to demonstrate your skills and track record in providing the service you're offering. Merely putting a sign on your door that says "Coach for Hire" isn't going to cut it (regrettably, some ambitious entrepreneurs fail to heed this advice. See Chapter 2 for more on this topic).

Target a Niche

Enrollment is easier and more effective when you target a specific niche than if you attempt to offer your services to any and all comers. People seek specialists to help them solve specific problems and achieve specific goals—something that you have experience with as a therapist. Getting coaching clients will depend more on whom you target and how than on your skills and experience. See Chapter 5 for more on this topic.

Design a Coaching Program

Designing a program for your niche makes your coaching services tangible, targeted, results-oriented, easier to market, and far more attractive. Remember, sell programs, not sessions! See Chapter 6 for more information.

Be Confident

This is your inner game. You can't expect your prospective clients to take the leap and trust you to help them get results if you're not completely and inspirationally confident in your ability to help them (without being grandiose, of course). Gaining this confidence authentically means becoming qualified by seeking training, practicing and honing your skills with real clients, getting coaching and mentoring to walk your talk and reach beyond your own limits (so you can help your clients reach beyond theirs), and getting the results you promise in your program with enough clients (along with their testimonials) that your confidence is backed up with solid evidence. This can be as simple as conducting a pilot program, or it might require years of research and development. Either way, once your program and your confidence in your services are in place, they will serve you well for many years to come.

Offer Something Irresistible

Effective enrollment requires designing an irresistible offer that compels your prospective clients to make a decision. They need a good reason to act now rather than put it off. If your program is a good fit for them, usually this decision will be "Yes." These reasons can include a deadline ("Enrollment window closes Friday at noon"), limited capacity ("Only two openings left"), discount ("$1,000 discount for signing up now"), bonus ("Sign up by Friday and include a friend or business partner at no extra charge"), choice ("Choose from the economical starter package or the full-featured platinum program"), and so on.

Be Skillful

Effective enrollment requires certain skills and strategies to connect with your prospects, build rapport, inspire excitement and confidence, and overcome obstacles to "Yes." We'll cover some effective strategies in this chapter, but the skills come with practice.

The Enrollment Conversation

Before enrollment can take place, you must engage your prospective clients in a conversation that lends itself to discussing their situation and your services. I call this the enrollment conversation. This conversation can be formal (e.g., when a prospective client makes an appointment with you to discuss your services), or it can be informal (e.g., a spontaneous chat at an airport). And remember, people generally *love* to talk about their goals, dreams, and aspirations. As a coach, you won't be perceived as pushy by encouraging people to share this aspect of themselves. (However, as a therapist, things are quite different—people are more reluctant, understandably, to share the darker aspects of their lives and personalities.)

All effective enrollment is the result of a one-to-one relationship and conversation, so here is an effective way to make them happen.

The Strategy Session

A strategy session designed to address the top goal of your niche can be a powerful way to motivate prospects to engage you in an enrollment conversation. For example, you could pitch your niche with something like: "Register now for your free 'Find Your Soul Mate in 90 Days' Strategy Session!"

Here are some guidelines to make an offer like this effective:

1. Do your market research and ensure that this is the top goal of your niche.

2. Ensure that your offer is composed in the language that your niche uses. For example, my niche uses the term *soul mate*, so they can instantly connect with that term. However, if they preferred to use the term *life partner*, then that's what I'd use. It's about them and their world, not me and mine (or you and yours).

3. Deliver your offer when your niche is most likely to respond favorably. This could occur during a presentation or seminar, after someone buys your book or audio program from your website, or at some other opportune time. Don't simply advertise it on your website and hope for the best.

4. Prequalify your prospects so you focus your time and effort on those folks most likely to hire you. You can prequalify prospects by having them fill out a short application, questionnaire, or assessment when making an appointment. Later on, when you have a full practice, you can even charge a fee for your strategy session and filter out less qualified prospects that way.

5. Vary your offer by season ("Find Your Soul Mate by Valentine's Day"), goal ("How to Be Attractive and Happy While Seeking Your Soul Mate"), niche ("Finding Your Soul Mate for the Over-50 Woman"), occasion ("Our First Anniversary Find Your Soul Mate Strategy Session"), and so on.

6. Limit your offer by providing a deadline and/or limited quantity. Your prospects are more likely to jump on your offer if they have a deadline, the shorter the better. Limiting the number you'll accept sends the message that you're selective, which makes you more attractive. And the truth is that you can't realistically handle too many strategy sessions, or you wouldn't have time to work with paying clients!

HOW TO CONDUCT A STRATEGY SESSION

When you meet with your prospects for their strategy sessions, I recommend the following five steps.

Step 1: Stoke Their Desire

Help your prospects explore and express their goals. Ask them "Why?" questions, such as:

- Why do you want to achieve this goal?
- Why is this important to you?
- Why have you chosen this goal instead of another?

These questions inspire prospects to talk about their situations and connect passionately to their goals. And the more passionate and emotionally connected they become, the easier the enrollment. Also, the answers supplied can provide you with valuable insights on how you'll actually help them realize their goals once they become clients! Be sure to ask, "How committed are you to this goal?" Use a 10-point scale, percentages, and so forth. Their answer will come in handy later.

Step 2: Stimulate Their Pain

Explore and stimulate the pain and frustration that your prospects experience because they haven't achieved their goals. Ask what they've tried in the past, what didn't work and why, what might be getting in their way, what lessons they've learned, how they might approach their goal differently, what it costs them to be where they are, and so on.

Step 3: Share the Solution

Establish your credibility, inspire hope and confidence, and position your services as the ideal solution for your prospect. If applicable, you can even share a true story (protecting names, of course) of how you helped another client in a similar situation. If you don't have a true client story, use something from your own life. (And if you don't have either type of success story, then you're probably not ready for this strategy and need more practice and experience helping people in your niche.)

Step 4: Get the First "Yes"

Based on the information you gained in the preceding steps, your judgment will tell you which of the following two responses is most appropriate:

> **Response A:** "I have a highly effective program for people just like you who want [insert the prospect's goal here]. Would you like to hear about it?" If the first three steps went well, your answer will almost always be "Yes."
>
> **Response B:** "I don't think you're a fit for my services, because [explain your reasons]. But would you like a couple of resources that I think might be helpful for you?"

As much as you might like to obtain a client, don't accept clients who aren't a good fit; it's not in their best interests or yours. It's better to be selective and leave the door open for more qualified clients than it is to fill your practice with anyone and everyone who will pay your fees.

Step 5: Get Hired!

This step involves three additional questions leading to getting hired. To begin, describe your coaching program, emphasizing the results and benefits that your market research told you were most desired by your target audience. Assume that your prospects need to clearly understand what's in it for them before covering nuts and bolts such as times, dates, and costs. Be sure they resonate with the results your program can deliver by asking: "Does that sound good to you?"

Here's an example from my world:

> "My Conscious Dating® Relationship Success Training for Singles program will help you become absolutely clear about who you are, what you want, and exactly how to get what you want in your life and relationships. I will help you develop a Conscious Dating plan with specific steps and strategies proven effective for singles like you, and I will personally support you to implement your Conscious Dating plan with confidence to be the chooser, avoid dating traps, and finally find the love of your life and the life that you love. Does that sound good to you?"

As you may have noticed, I didn't use the word *coaching* in there at all! Instead, I focused on benefits and outcomes, which are precisely what prospects want, need, and expect to have in order to say "Yes."

After describing how your coaching program can help your prospects and learning that it indeed sounds good to them, ask: "Do you have any questions about this program?" Chances are, as you can expect, you'll be asked about fees and other details. This is fine, because your prospects are going into that territory of their own free will; you aren't *dragging* them in there by inundating them with information before they're ready for it.

After answering all their questions, summarize the results and benefits of your program and ask: "Are you ready to get started?"

This question will result either in your final "Yes" and you've got a client (congratulations) or in the prospect starting to pull back with another response, which I'll discuss next.

Here's a recap you can copy and use as a guide:

Step 1: Stoke their desire.
Step 2: Stimulate their pain.
Step 3: Share the solution.
Step 4: Get the first "Yes."
> Say that you have a highly effective program for reaching the prospect's goal and ask: "Would you like to hear about it?"

Step 5: Get hired!
> Describe your program and ask: "Does that sound good to you?"
> If yes, ask: "Do you have any questions about this program?"
> Answer any questions and ask: "Are you ready to get started?"

OVERCOMING OBJECTIONS

Objections are the statements your prospect makes that are not "Yes," but they're not "No," either.

My insight into why this phenomenon occurs? Plain, old-fashioned fear. Folks can simply become afraid and have all sorts of self-doubts going through their minds, such as "Will this really work for me?" "Do I deserve happiness and success?" "Can I really do this?" and so on. Their fear of failure *and* their fear of success will often be rationalized with phrases like "I need to think about this" or "I don't have the time" or "I'm not sure I can afford this right now." Here's a perspective on these objections that I really like:

> *"Every client objection can be viewed as the very reason for why they should commit to coaching with you."*
> —JOHN BRIDGES, NATURAL PERSUASION TECHNOLOGIES

Fortunately, you have a very simple and powerful tool to help your prospective clients overcome fear: *desire*. They've already told you how much they desire their goal and how committed they are to it. Now all you need to do is back up and repeat step 1. It's that simple.

Of course, some objections aren't based on fear, and these aren't hard to detect, especially by a seasoned helping professional. For example, you might hear: "I'd like to, but I can't afford it right now." And after you discuss their financial situation and agree that, yes, money is an issue and a legitimate obstacle, you can respond in a variety of ways:

- Refer them to an appropriate low-cost or no-cost support resource.
- Offer to stay in touch and set a future date for follow-up.
- Offer them a scholarship application (see "Scholarships and Pro Bono Services" under "Creative Marketing Strategies" in Chapter 7).
- Ask, "Who in your life cares about your success and would be willing to help you participate in this program?" (see "Sponsors" under "Creative Marketing Strategies" in Chapter 7).

All of these are respectful, viable responses that often will result in your prospect finding a creative solution to joining your program, either now or in the future.

Ask for Referrals

Toward the end of your strategy session, ask for a referral by inquiring: "Whom do you know who would benefit from this program?"

Be prepared with your referral packet (see "Primary Marketing Strategy #3" in Chapter 7), and provide an extra copy (or several). You can even go so far as to ask your prospect to call a referral right then and there and introduce you. I've seen this strategy work very, very well.

The 24-Hour Challenge

I designed this exercise many years ago for the participants in my practice-building programs, and it was 100% successful. It was inspired by my friend and former business partner Marv Cohen. A week before the start of each class or workshop, he would identify how many empty seats needed to be filled and would get on the telephone until they were booked. I asked him how he did this, and he said he simply called his prospect list to follow up and connect with them. More often than not the conversation turned to their goals and our program and they decided to enroll—no hard sell at all!

So here's how it starts. Set your mind-set and intention by pretending you're on a reality TV show and you will win a million dollars if you get one new paying client in the next 24 hours.

What would you do? If one million dollars could be yours tomorrow if you got just one new client, you would overcome your fear and resistance and get creative!

While there are many possible ways to do this, the easiest and most successful way is to simply get on the telephone, start at the top of your prospect list (or people you know), and work your way down until you get a client.

Here are three suggested steps:

Step 1: Gather the contact information of everyone you know.

Dig into drawers for forgotten business cards, find old address books, look through the yellow pages for colleagues you forgot you knew, and collect your e-mail addresses and website favorites. At some point, you'll want to compile all these people into a database that you can use for your internal marketing, but for now you just want to collect enough prospects to keep you busy on the telephone until you succeed in getting one new paying client from the list.

Step 2: Write a script for leaving an enticing voice mail.

Assume that you will mostly be speaking to voice mail instead of a human being. What can you say that will compel a call back? Get creative! If you know that their situation and goals fit your program, how about offering them your strategy session?

Step 3: When you eventually get them on the telephone, speak in a casual, relaxed, friendly tone of voice.

Don't be in a hurry, don't push, and don't be attached to any particular outcome. The attitude to adopt is that you're just calling to connect, you have all the time in the world, and catching up with them would be the most fun and pleasurable thing for you to do in this moment. Your goal is to get them to talk and to naturally enter into a coaching conversation with them as if it were a strategy session.

Chat about how you know each other; ask them about their situation, needs, goals, and challenges. Reflect back what you're hearing and focus on the goal or challenge related to your specialty. If they appear to resonate to your identification of their goal, proceed with step 1 of conducting a strategy session and go as far as they are willing.

And that's all there is to it!

If you push through your resistance and fear, you *will* get a client—and a lot sooner than you think!

And if you can get one client, you can get two, and three, and so on. You will have proven to yourself that you can get clients whenever you want to, which will raise your confidence and ability to enroll other clients, and will guarantee your success in your private practice.

CHAPTER NINE

Building a Successful Coaching Business

Becoming an entrepreneur.

How to get paid what you're worth.

Promoting client loyalty and longevity.

Maximizing your private practice income.

How to have fun, play large, and retire smiling.

SEVEN HABITS OF HIGHLY SUCCESSFUL PRACTITIONERS

Only a small percentage of helping professionals are able to reach their financial goals through full-time private practice. The others (the majority) must supplement their income by working with insurance companies, accepting part-time employment, discounting their rates, and doing other things that, frankly, they *don't* want to do.

What these helping professionals overlook is that a private practice is an *entrepreneurial venture* requiring skills and strategies that they don't teach in graduate school. And furthermore, these are skills that, in my experience, don't come naturally to most helping professionals. By and large, folks who are called to helping professions (like therapy) aren't interested in or energized by *business*. In fact, some hate it! This attitude, however, is a barrier that must be overcome. I've found that highly successful coaches are the ones who embrace their inner entrepreneur and share the following seven characteristics.

1. **Passionate.** Highly successful coaches love their work, are so excited by it that they would do it for free, and have no thought or intention of retirement. They truly could not *imagine* doing anything else, and consider themselves lucky to have the best job in the world. Their passion is easily expressed, and very attractive to their potential clients.

2. **Positive.** These coaches have a *can-do* attitude. They truly believe in themselves and trust that they will find a way around obstacles to survive and thrive, and thus are able to effectively empower their clients to be positive as well. While they may experience fears and doubts, they assume abundance instead of scarcity.

3. **Entrepreneurial.** While most coaches understandably wish to focus on serving their clients and resist the business and marketing aspects of their practice, successful coaches enjoy the challenge of pioneering a successful business that is an expression of their gifts, mission, and purpose.

4. **Play large.** Highly successful coaches are always expanding by growing themselves and their practices. They desire to play as large as they can, and take every opportunity to do so. They grow impatient with the status quo, and are always in motion seeking to maximize their time, energy, opportunities, and resources.

5. **Creative.** Highly successful coaches build on what they've learned and are excited by developing their own approaches to their work that express their gifts, talents, and perspectives. They typically enjoy the thought of writing a book or developing a program that would make a unique and powerful contribution to the world.

6. **Service-oriented.** Highly successful coaches truly wish to make a difference in the world, and are grateful for the opportunity to be of service to their clients. While they may have their financial goals, they wish to practice right livelihood, and it's more important for them to fulfill their mission and purpose than it is to be financially successful.

7. **Walk the talk.** Highly successful coaches believe in the value of their work and are enthusiastic clients as well. They put time and effort into developing themselves and building the life that they really want while they are making a living helping others do so. They have walked in their clients' shoes, and continue to do so.

Top Five Strategies to Maximize Your Private Practice Income

I strongly believe that "if you take care of your business, your business will take care of you." You rely on your practice to pay your bills, prepare for retirement, send your kids to college, and provide you a comfortable living—all *hugely* important goals. Here are five ways you can help your coaching business take very good care of you and provide the financial security you want and deserve while you're making a difference in the world.

Strategy 1: Give Yourself a Raise Every Year

When was the last time you raised your fees? If you look around, you'll see that prices go up constantly, and other professionals, businesses, and services raise their fees accordingly as their costs go up. I'm amazed at how many private-practice professionals charge the same amount year after year and are surprised years later when they end up making far less than their colleagues. Here's a strategy for you:

   Step 1: Choose an anniversary date for your practice. Just like your birthday and your wedding anniversary, your practice deserves to be honored and celebrated once a year (at least!). Go out to dinner and toast your practice, buy your practice some new furnishings, and mark the occasion for the significant event that it is. Open up your calendar and choose an anniversary date. This can be the day you were licensed, the first of the year, tax day—any day of the year that you would like to designate as the anniversary date of your practice.

Step 2: Determine your new rate. Bump up your rate significantly. It almost doesn't matter what your new rate is as long as you are examining it and raising it each year.

Step 3: Modify your paperwork. Update your documentation and anywhere else your rate is stated with your new rate.

Step 4: Notify current clients 30 days in advance. Do *not* be tempted to keep your old rate for your current clients, some of whom might continue working with you for years to come. Don't worry about losing clients if you raise your rate, as this almost never happens. Your clients fully understand that as the cost of everything goes up, your rate needs to go up as well. Any client who chooses to terminate because of a rate increase was getting ready to leave anyway and can be replaced by a client who is better able to benefit from your services and will be happy to pay your full fee.

Step 5: *Do it* and never look back!

Strategy 2: Private Pay Only!

I don't know *any* private-practice professional who wants to deal with third-party reimbursement. Coaching is not medically necessary and is ineligible for medical insurance reimbursement, anyway (please don't be tempted to bill using V codes or "adjustment disorder"). Coaching is effective only when the client is invested by paying out-of-pocket, which is better for the client and better for you. Here are some strategies:

- **Get a merchant account to accept credit cards.** You will get far more clients and generate far more income if you accept credit cards.
- **Bill by the month or by the program.** Don't bill by the session. Even though it's the familiar model, you don't want each session to be a buying decision; change takes time and you want your clients to commit to working with you as long as it takes to achieve their goals. If you have a high-dollar coaching program, you can split the cost into monthly payments for those who can't afford the full cost up front.

- **Set up recurring billing.** Have your clients sign an agreement giving you permission to bill their credit cards each month for your services. In some systems this can be set up to be automatic. Then, once your clients make the decision to hire you they can concentrate on their coaching, and your fees automatically show up on their credit card statements until they decide otherwise.

Strategy 3: No Sliding Scale or Discounts!

I believe I've emphasized this enough and provided viable and more effective options to convince you that negotiating your fees is unnecessary and unproductive for you and your clients. You will earn far more when you value your services enough to charge the full fee all the time to everyone, and will attract and serve far more qualified clients when you do so.

Strategy 4: Groups

Leverage your time and earn far more per hour with group programs. Most coaching niches are actually served more effectively with groups, as participants are able to support and coach each other as well as receive your support and coaching.

Strategy 5: Multiple Revenue Streams

You will earn far more by diversifying your services and sources of revenue to include:

- Passive income (affiliate programs appropriate for your niche).
- Products, such as books, CDs, and videos, both those created by you and those you recommend (through affiliate programs) created by others.
- Packages: Bundle your individual and group services as well as products into "Silver," "Gold," and "Platinum" packages. You will earn more per client and provide more effective services when clients benefit from more than one service.
- Joint ventures: Collaborate with complementary professionals who provide services your niche needs but that you don't provide.

HOW TO GET PAID WHAT YOU'RE WORTH

Many helping professionals feel guilty about charging for their services. Here's why I think this happens:

- **Student mentality:** You feel as if you have a lot to learn, and haven't yet mastered your craft.
- **Charity mentality:** You want to be of service and help others, and have a hard time forcing people to pay for it.
- **Empathic mentality:** Your fee feels expensive to you, so you charge only what you, personally, would be comfortable paying.
- **Antiprofit mentality:** You dislike and distrust the business-oriented profit motive.
- **Money issues:** You are uncomfortable with money, don't like dealing with money, and feel like you don't have enough money—yet don't want to put effort into making money.

Do you recognize yourself in any of these descriptions? The first step to getting paid what you're worth is to identify what's getting in your way.

Here are some reasons to charge a significant fee for your services:

o **Results:** The effectiveness of your services is directly related to the level of commitment of your clients, which is tied closely to how much they pay out of their pockets to work with you.

o **Selectivity:** You attract clients who understand and value the benefit of your services and working with you, and avoid clients that hire you because you're "affordable."

o **Sustainability:** Your ability to help others depends on your ability to earn a sustainable living. You aren't helping anyone by struggling financially and seeking other part-time or full-time work to get by.

o **Reciprocity:** A good working relationship is equal and reciprocal. You will prioritize doing your best for clients who pay your full fee, and will unconsciously treat clients paying discounted fees differently (and these clients will feel different as well); this just can't be avoided. When you feel trapped into accepting fees lower than you feel you're worth, you can end up resenting your clients and burning out.

o **Funding community service:** If you are making a comfortable living, you can afford to provide pro bono services, give free seminars and workshops to low-income populations, donate a portion of your income to nonprofit organizations, and so forth.

o **Making a larger difference:** When you charge what you're worth, the more people you help, the more money you make. The more money you make, the more people you can help. Earning a significant income is key to making the difference you want to make in the world.

So how much should you charge? Here are five strategies for figuring that out:

1. **Double your comfort level.** Take the figure you're comfortable paying and double it.
2. **Stretch your clients.** Knowing the demographics of your niche, charge a bit above what they would pay for similar services elsewhere, for two reasons: You'll be perceived to be a better choice because you're more expensive, and they will benefit more from a service they have to stretch to pay for.
3. **One-up your competition.** As in the preceding guideline, when you charge more than your colleagues, you're perceived to be worth more.
4. **Charge for results.** Instead of charging by the hour, session, or month, price your service for what the *result* is worth to the client. How much is an hour of coaching worth? How much is achieving an important goal worth? These two figures will be very different.
5. **Sell programs, not sessions!** Charge for your coaching program tailored for your niche; do not focus on the number or length of sessions. Focus on the benefits and results of your program, not labels like "coaching."

PROMOTING CLIENT LOYALTY AND LONGEVITY

The key to a successful coaching practice is to *continually* measure and prove the value and benefits of working with you. Coaching is results-oriented, and measuring results gives you necessary feedback about the effectiveness of your work with your client, and proves to the client that you are committed to results. You don't want your client to wonder, "Is this coaching working for me?" At regular intervals (monthly or at least quarterly), you want to measure progress as objectively as possible. Here are three ways:

> **Option 1: Goal tracking.** At the beginning of your coaching relationship you established goals. Measuring progress can be as simple as reviewing progress toward those goals, as well as toward new goals established over the course of coaching.
>
> **Option 2: Checklist.** The people in your niche have similar needs, goals, and challenges, and they go through similar stages and steps and experience similar obstacles in accomplishing the results you are helping them achieve. What are they? Make and organize a list, and you have a checklist!
>
> **Option 3: Assessment.** Your checklist can be expanded into an assessment by organizing the items into categories and providing a rating system in which each item is scored and the scores can be added up for a final tally. These scores can also be graphed, providing your clients with a visual representation of their progress. Make sure you administer this assessment at the beginning of coaching to get a baseline. This assessment is also a great enrollment tool when used during the enrollment conversation to identify areas of strength and weakness for goal setting, making a convincing case for the need for your coaching services.

EPILOGUE: HAVE FUN, PLAY LARGE, AND RETIRE SMILING

If you're like me, you pursued a career as a helping professional because you wanted (and still want) to make a positive difference in the world. And, if you're even more like me, you want to live comfortably, send your kids to college, have fun, grow old with your soul mate, live a full and meaningful life, and leave a legacy. This is my definition of success.

Frankly, I never thought I would stop being a therapist, and I did. I never thought I would write a book or start an institute, and I did. These twists and turns in my career tell me that life is full of surprises, so I've learned to expect the unexpected and be open to where my journey leads.

Though I don't know exactly what to expect in the next 20 years of my life, it gives me great comfort and pleasure to know that if and when I retire, I'll retire smiling. This is my wish for you as well, and the vision that has inspired the creation of this book. Enjoy it, share it, and *use it* on your path to success . . . wherever it leads!

Appendix A

Selected resources for building your coaching business

- Hosting conference calls and teleseminars: http://www.easyseminar.com
- International Coach Federation: http://www.coachfederation.org
- Relationship Coaching Institute: http://www.relationshipcoachinginstitute.com
- Institute for Life Coach Training: http://www.lifecoachtraining.com
- Autoresponders: http://www.coachautoresponder.com
- Article directory: http://www.ezinearticles.com
- Automated article submission: http://www.easyarticlesyndication.com
- Copy writing for print and Internet: http://www.getresultswithwords.com
- Do-it-yourself website solution: http://www.easywordpresssolutions.com
- Websites done for you: http://www.BestTherapistCoachWebsites.com

- Practice management console: http://www.managemycoachingpractice.com
- Accept credit cards: http://www.bestepaymentsolution.com
- Shopping cart with affiliate program: http://www.bestcoachshoppingcart.com
- Newsletters done for you: http://www.bestcoachnewsletters.com
- Marketing help for coaches and therapists: http://www.bestcoachmarketing.com
- Marketing and building a successful coaching practice: http://www.milliondollarpractice.net
- Comprehensive practice-building information: http://www.privatepracticemarketingonabudget.com
- Effective, ethical client enrollment: http://www.naturalclientenrollmentstrategies.com
- Develop signature audio/CD program: http://www.privatepracticemagic.com
- VoIP (can be used with regular telephones): http://www.magicjack.com
- Headsets and telephones: http://www.headsets.com
- Find an affordable virtual assistant: http://www.findmyva.net
- Find an affordable webmaster: http://www.findmywebmaster.com
- Free audio series "How to Earn Six Figures as an Expert Who Speaks": http://www.relationshipcoachinginstitute.com/speakingbiz.htm
- Free quick-start program "Using Conference Calls to Grow Your Business": http://www.easyseminar.com/quickstart.html
- Free comprehensive resource bank for private practice professionals: http://www.milliondollarpractice.net/resource-bank

Appendix B

14 Compelling reasons to use a professional coach

The coaching relationship is unique and powerful, and can help people find fulfillment in their lives and relationships. The following are 14 important reasons to use a professional coach, any one of which is compelling enough to persuade people to get their very own coach.

1. **You highly value your quality of life.**
   You prioritize building a fulfilling personal and professional life and relationships. You realize that your success and quality of life are directly connected to your goals and outcomes in achieving them.

2. **You are committed to success.**
   You are serious and intentional about having a fulfilling life partnership, family, business, and community.

3. **You want results.**
   Working with a coach can move you farther, faster, than you can on your own.

4. **You are willing to learn.**

    You realize that you don't know what you don't know, and your future success may depend on access to new skills and knowledge.

5. **You are ready for action.**

    Using a coach can be the most effective means of translating knowledge into practice. One of the most indispensable roles of a coach is to help you use what you already know to make effective choices and take the actions necessary to be successful.

6. **You are open to mentoring and support.**

    A coach helps you to use your life and relationships to evolve and develop skills critical to your business success and personal fulfillment. The process of self-discovery and learning about how to make successful choices in real life cannot be effectively self-taught or obtained from a book or tape.

7. **You want fulfillment.**

    You do not want to settle for less or risk preventable failure, and you are willing to give yourself the gift of the support and technology needed to be successful.

8. **You want to be true to yourself.**

    A coach helps keep you honest with yourself, helps neutralize any tendency you may have to settle for less than you really want, and is good for providing reality checks and being a sounding board.

9. **You want to be proactive.**

    A coach helps you solve problems while they are still small.

10. **You want to go beyond your limits.**

    A coach holds your highest vision for you beyond your fears and perceived limitations, and helps you overcome your obstacles and challenges.

11. **You want to take responsibility.**

    A coach helps you take responsibility for the quality of your life and relationships so that you can create them the way you want.

12. **You want to live authentically.**

    Today's world is filled with challenges to finding and staying on your highest path, telling your truth, and making choices that are best for you. A coach helps you identify and live the life you really want, and be more of the person you really are and want to be.

13. **You want balance in your life.**

    Your life is filled with opportunities and conflicting choices. You recognize the importance of creating and maintaining balance in your life and relationships, including the ones you have with yourself and your higher power.

14. **You want new possibilities for yourself.**

    A coach helps you to continually discover and implement new and more fulfilling possibilities for your life and relationships.

No one is successful alone. Working with a professional coach helps people go farther, faster, than they can by themselves. When they find a coach who specializes in their particular needs and goals, they have nothing to lose and everything to gain!

Appendix C

A short history of coaching for clinicians

PATRICK WILLIAMS, EdD, MCC

Founder, Institute for Life Coach Training

Coaching is an important new profession that developed from the fields of counseling, consulting, adult learning, and other helping strategies in human development. The coaching relationship is very distinct from just using coaching skills, some of which are common to other helping professions. Coaching is a cocreated conversation to empower the receiver of the coaching in which an *expert/client paradigm* is intentionally absent. It is a unique professional relationship in which a client explores with the coach (over time) how to live life more fully and "on purpose."

Coaching has a unique paradigm, one focused on growth and empowerment, but much of the foundation of coaching goes back many decades and even centuries. The drive to pursue life improvement, personal development, and the exploration of meaning began with early Greek society (in the Western tradition). This is reflected in Socrates' famous quote, "The unexamined life is not worth living."

Since then, people have developed many ways of examining their lives. In modern society there is less need to focus on the pursuit of basic human needs—such as food and shelter—enabling us to pay attention to higher needs such as self-actualization, fulfillment, and spiritual connection.

Coaching today is seen as a new phenomenon, but as a field it borrows from and builds on theories and research from related fields such as psychology and philosophy. So coaching is *a multidisciplinary, multitheory* synthesis and application of applied behavioral change. As coaching evolved in the public arena it began to incorporate accepted theories of behavioral change as the evidence base for this new helping relationship. However, in recent years, more and more research has been done, and evidence-based theories have been developed to begin creating a body of knowledge and evidence that coaching can call its own.

Contributions From Psychology

What has the field of psychology brought to coaching and what are the major influences? I would propose that there have been four major forces in psychological theory since the emergence of psychology in 1879 as a social science. These four forces are Freudian, behavioral, humanistic, and transpersonal. Both the Freudian and behavioral models grew out of biology and were focused on pathology and how to cure it. The humanistic approaches of Carl Rogers and Abraham Maslow were a response to the pathological model; they attempted to make space in psychology for those elements of being human that create health and happiness. Finally, the transpersonal movement arose in the late 1960s in a further attempt to include more of what allows human beings to function at their best. Its focus was on mind, body, and spirit and included studies and experiences of states of consciousness, transcendence, and what Eastern traditions and practices had to teach Western theorists and practitioners. A more recent approach, the integral model of Ken Wilber and others, is emerging and may become a fifth force, integrating all that has come before and offering a holistic and even multilevel view of the various modalities for understanding human development and our desire to evolve mentally, physically, spiritually, and socially.

In recent years, several other approaches have arisen as adaptations of one or more of the original four and have been taken up by many coaches. Cognitive-behavioral psychology grew from a mix of the behavioral and humanistic schools. I say this because much of cognitive psychology embodied wisdom and learning from behaviorism and even operant conditioning. But when the humanistic aspect was included, it became a way to use those techniques and theories of change to increase *choice* for the individual. In coaching, then, you can utilize what we know about shifting the mind-set and behaviors by using a process of inquiry and powerful questions that guide the client to understanding her or his ability to respond rather than react to personal situations. Responding comes from viewing the multiple choices available in cognition and behavior rather than just reacting habitually.

Positive psychology builds on two key principles from humanistic psychology: a nonmechanistic perspective and a view of possibility as opposed to pathology as the essential approach to the client. Humanistic psychology arose as a counterpoint to the view of Freudian psychology and behaviorism that people could be viewed as products of unconscious and conditioned responses. Humanistic psychology arose to promote the emphasis on personal growth and the importance of *beingness* and the phenomenology of the human experience. Along with each revolution in psychology, a changing image of human nature has evolved along with greater insights into how to effectively work with people.

Looking back at the psychological theorists of the 20th century who laid the groundwork for the emergence and evolution of personal and professional coaching is important for understanding the origins of our profession. It is important for professional coaches to know that quality coach training and education are based in a multidimensional model of human development and communication that has drawn from the best of humanistic psychology, positive psychology, integral psychology, and other models in this field. Coaching also draws from fields such as organizational development, adult learning theory, and systems theory.

Many of the same techniques that originated in clinical psychology are useful in assisting clients to reframe their experience and to discover their strengths. These techniques include powerful questions; guided imagery (psychosynthesis); empty chair technique (Gestalt therapy); time lines and future pacing (neuro-linguistic programming [NLP]); and even techniques and theory from transactional analysis (Eric Berne), client-centered counseling (Carl Rogers), and life-stage awareness (Carl Jung, Frederic Hudson, Carol Gilligan, and Robert Kegan, among others).

THE CURSE OF THE MEDICAL MODEL

Somewhere along the way, the helping professions (spearheaded by clinical psychology) adopted, or were co-opted by, the medical model. It's important to understand how this view is in direct opposition to the coaching model. The medical model sees the client as being ill, as a patient with a diagnosis in need of treatment or symptom relief. While there clearly are some serious mental illnesses that benefit from clinical psychology or skillful psychotherapy, many people in the past were treated and labeled for what were really problems in living—situations or circumstances that did not need a diagnosis or assumption of pathology. In the past, people seeking personal growth typically had nowhere to turn but to therapists, seminars, or self-help books. Sadly, many of these seminars and books also were problem-focused rather than looking forward for the powerful strategies of healthy life design.

Today, many clinicians find themselves on a dead-end street blocked by a corporate managed health care system where the main concern is financial profit, not mental health delivery. Unfortunately, most diagnoses pathologized people who weren't really mentally ill. These diagnoses became part of the clients' permanent medical records, leading to embarrassment, insurance rejection, and other unnecessary problems. I believe society is ready for a coaching model in which a relationship is sought to create a future—not to get over a past—and certainly not to get labeled with a diagnosis for their effort.

I believe psychotherapy and counseling can effectively treat diagnosable mental illnesses (although the research on this point is often inconclusive). However, these longer-term treatments (if you expect insurance to foot the bills) are often viewed as too expensive. Increasingly, the benefits of a relationship in which change and insight occur over time are not supported in the medical model. The counseling professions, in my opinion, fell into a trap after adopting the medical model and third-party payment for services. Now, in order to survive, counselors and therapists are reducing fees, and psychologists are even trying to obtain prescription privileges for psychotropic drugs, moving further into the medical arena. G. W. Albee says that psychologists (and therefore other therapists) have "sold their souls to the Devil: the disease model of mental disorders" (1998, pp. 189–194).

CONCLUSION

The core of the coaching profession is grounded in sound academic and scholarly theories that preceded coaching, and it will be strengthened by the validation of theories and evidence-based research as the profession moves forward. All the amazing tools that have grown out of modern psychology support coaches in assisting clients to create change as desired by our clients. As the recent emergence of positive psychology demonstrates, new developments become available all the time.

The hallmarks of coaching are its synthesis of tools from other fields and its proclivity for innovation. With all of the research going on today, coaching is developing its own evidence-based theories. It has borrowed from what has gone before, much as psychologists borrowed from philosophers. As coaching grows as a profession, it is developing its own research base of effective strategies and tools within the unique relationship that is the coaching alliance. This short survey of the history of coaching is an attempt to glean the practical from the scientific. How do all the knowledge and theories inform your coaching business? How do you know what skills work best and also fit your style? Knowing that the skill sets and competencies of coaching are not invented out of thin air adds credibility to an emerging profession, and finding practical uses for the theories in coaching relationships makes a difference in people's lives.

Professional coaches support their clients in walking a new path toward desired change. They do so by bringing *multiple perspectives* to their work and appreciating the unique gifts and strengths of each individual client. At the same time, they can see how the client's work fits within the context of how human beings generally develop over the course of a life span.

I believe coaching has arisen as a profession because of the shortage of real listening in our society today and the lack of true connection that many people experience. These factors arise from the socioeconomic conditions of rapid change, technological advances, and the instant availability of information. Carl Rogers once said that counseling was like buying a friend; hiring a coach is similar. But, of course, it is much more than that. A coach is a partner who is hired to assist the client in going for greatness in any and all domains of the client's life. People may not always *need* a coach, but I believe they do always *deserve* a coach.

REFERENCE

Albee, G. W. (1998). Fifty years of clinical psychology: Selling our soul to the devil. *Applied and Preventive Psychology, 7*, 189–194.

Appendix D

Six stages of client readiness for change

Patrick Williams, EdD, MCC

Founder, Institute for Life Coach Training

James Prochaska's theory of *readiness for change* can help coaches understand where they can most effectively enter the client's landscape of living. Prochaska's work emerged from the field of addiction counseling and research on which behavior and style by the counselor would best match the stage of the client's readiness for change. Prochaska, Norcross, and DiClemente (1994) identified six well-defined, time-based stages that clients move through, although not necessarily in a linear way. This model can also be quite useful in coaching as a way to apply the appropriate strategies necessary to support the client's movement through change and toward the desired state or behavior.

What follows is a coaching example using the six stages. In it, the client's goals for coaching are to improve his or her health and begin an exercise routine.

STAGE 1: PRECONTEMPLATION

At the precontemplation stage, the client actually is not yet considering making a change. Clients sometimes are unaware of the need for a change or are unaware of their current patterns or behaviors. If the coach sees that the client seems to be at this stage, the client is not ready to make big changes. When coaching a client at this stage, the initial exploration and assessment phases of coaching can be critical.

Clients who want to improve their health are already beyond this stage. It is not as if precontemplators cannot think of a solution—it is that they do not identify a problem. The client referred to earlier has already identified a problem and has reframed it as a goal: to improve his or her health and begin an exercise routine. Coaches are unlikely to find clients at the precontemplation stage, unless perhaps they have been sent by their employer for a problem they have not identified on their own. Sometimes, however, a client comes to a coach for one reason and something else emerges over time. In this case, the client may be at the precontemplation stage around a particular issue.

It is important for coaches using Prochaska's model to recognize that the stage is related to the specific issue; a client may be at several different stages for several different goals, which requires flexibility on the part of the coach. The coach may be working with a client on work issues or on improving fulfillment in relationships when the client goes to the doctor and discovers his or her cholesterol and blood pressure are high, and the doctor recommends that the patient focus on his or her health. Here, the client has received *assessment data* from the doctor. Sometimes assessment data are utilized in coaching. These can be formal, as from a plethora of available personality assessments, or informal, as in the initial client interview or use of the wheel of life model. In either case, a coaching strategy for moving a client from precontemplation to the second stage, contemplation, is to use assessment data. A coach would be looking to see if the client is accepting the information or denying that a problem exists that might need to be addressed.

STAGE 2: CONTEMPLATION

Clients at the contemplation stage are considering making a change and also may find they are quite ambivalent about it, or they may not know what to do to make the change. They can endlessly weigh the pros and cons but not actually decide to take action. The coach can assist the client at this stage to examine how the current situation and the client's habits, behaviors, and patterns work for and against him or her. For this client who wants to improve health and initiate exercise, the coach might ask: "What kind of exercise do you most enjoy?" or "What will be the result if you keep things as they are and don't make any changes?" or "What are the pros and cons for you of initiating a regular exercise program?" The client may be a busy executive who travels quite often and feels time-pressured. If so, the coach's role might be to help the client examine the consequences of allowing work to overtake time and schedule to the detriment of health. In addition, the coach helps the client explore the motivation to change versus the motivation to keep things as they are.

This is where a coach could use Perls's empty chair technique with the client. The coach would ask the client to map out the pros and cons of two poles of an issue—in this case, exercise program or no exercise program—and to identify the positive and negative aspects of each side. Then, the coach works with the client to have one part of himself or herself take the pro side of the desire and then sit in another chair and give voice to the other side. This technique is a nonthreatening way to give voice to the inner dialogue that is just beneath the surface. The coach is an ally to help the client find a pathway for moving forward with more clarity and commitment. This technique of giving voice to different parts of the client is most often seen today as working with the *gremlin* or *inner critic* in coaching. The use of the empty chair technique could serve the client very well in not only making the internal dialogue external, but also in having some lively fun while they are at it. This does not have to be applied as it would in a psychotherapy situation but instead could be done in a light-hearted but profoundly insightful manner in coaching.

STAGE 3: PREPARATION

At the preparation stage, the client is preparing to change—gathering information, assembling resources, checking out possibilities, and preparing to act. This is where the focus on accountability in coaching can be paramount. The coach can help the client discover resources, identify what is needed, and cocreate possibilities and choices and, with them, the willingness and desire to move forward.

Helping the client move from contemplation to preparation can be a significant accomplishment in itself. The client begins to overcome the inertia that characterized the previous stage, where the only action was *thinking* about action. Coaches sometimes feel that they have failed if their client does not jump into action. Instead, it is important to recognize that the preparation stage is critical. The coach's work is to help initiate change; for the client seeking health, for example, it is researching on the Internet local resources for health clubs, trainers, classes, or other health and fitness opportunities. This *is* movement—although sometimes the coach who is unfamiliar with Prochaska's work does not see it that way. With this model in mind, a coach can maintain the patience to allow the client to move through each stage, knowing that the client's ultimate success will be better ensured if each stage is addressed fully according to the client's unique needs.

STAGE 4: ACTION

This is the classic stage where the client actually takes action, practices new behaviors, and tries new things. The coach's role is to ensure that clients' actions are congruent with who they are and what they want. The work in the initial three stages to identify their own ways of taking action is empowering for clients. The ideas for action do not come from the coach's preconceptions or advice but, instead, have resulted from the cocreative process of coaching. This client's actions may include hiring a personal trainer, buying a piece of exercise equipment and using it, setting up a regular workout schedule, changing his or her diet, and so on.

STAGE 5: MAINTENANCE

At the maintenance stage, the client has maintained the chosen actions long enough to have created new habits and integrated them into the rest of his or her life. This usually indicates that new habits are being installed and are likely to last; coaching at this time continues to acknowledge and endorse the changes. The client's alliance with the coach increases the likelihood of enduring success, particularly with clients who may not have been successful at maintaining change in the past. If the client slips back into old habits or if circumstances change, the coach can assist the client to reset goals or recalibrate actions.

Just as in car maintenance, occasional tune-ups and adjustments are needed to address the current situation. Clients sometimes believe that they can consistently maintain actions over time, no matter what. Yet life brings changes. This client may develop a health issue that requires changing the preferred way of exercise and this may be more difficult than expected. As another example, a new child in the family may require realignment of the client's use of time and energy.

STAGE 6: TERMINATION

Prochaska used this term because it reflects the fact that the client no longer requires a programmatic approach to the behavior that needed changing. The new behavior has become a natural part of the person's life, and it happens without much thought on his or her part. For our client, the exercise program has simply become a part of what the client does each week—a new habit, perhaps even a new joyful habit.

In coaching, stage 6 may not mean an end to the coaching per se. It may simply mean that the coaching will no longer focus on a particular goal—it has been terminated, so to speak. Some clients may feel that they have achieved their coaching goals. The coach helps the client recognize when ongoing maintenance coaching or coaching for new issues will be of benefit. It is important to keep in mind that *change is a process, not an event*. On any desired change, the client may cycle through these stages in a nonlinear fashion. These steps are not linear—they are spiral. For example, coaches commonly see a pattern in which the client commits to taking action by the next session but instead moves back from the action stage to the contemplation stage. The coach's role is to support the client's movement through the cycle and to accept the client wherever he or she is in the moment.

REFERENCE

Prochaska, J. O., Norcross, J. C., & DiClemente, C. C. (1994). *Changing for good: A revolutionary six-stage program for overcoming bad habits and moving your life forward*. New York, NY: HarperCollins.

Appendix E

Beyond psychotherapy: working outside the medical model

JOHN A. MARTIN, PHD

"Do you take insurance?" is a question I often get from prospective clients, although less frequently these days.

My answer, in a nutshell, is "I don't." In fact, I resigned from the last of my managed care/preferred provider panels over 20 years ago. This essay explains the reasoning behind my decision, and how my practice as a licensed psychologist has evolved since then.

First, a word on the historical context. In the 1960s, with the advent of state licensing of psychologists, our incentives to formulate the American Psychiatric Association's *Diagnostic and Statistical Manual of Mental Disorders* (*DSM*)–based diagnoses changed radically. Psychologists fought hard for parity with psychiatrists, and eventually won the right to be reimbursed by third parties (insurance companies) for the "medically necessary treatment of mental and nervous disease." For a while, nearly everyone with insurance that covered psychological services had complete freedom of choice: Clients chose a psychiatrist, psychologist, or other licensed mental health professional more or less without restriction, and bills submitted for reimbursement were routinely paid with minimal rigmarole by insurance companies up to the contract's limits. This was a huge benefit to psychologists like me, although for some of us the cost of this change was also substantial: In order to participate, psychologists, including those of us who were ill-disposed to do so, were required to start thinking of clients and their problems in terms of psychiatric diagnoses à la the *DSM*.

Whether or not we ordinarily thought of clients in the context of mental illnesses and disease classifications, participation in the third-party reimbursement system demanded that each client be labeled with a diagnosis, which in turn became part of their permanent medical record. The insurance companies were relatively uninvolved in diagnoses and treatment plans. Diagnostic codes were shared with insurers, but details about cases were kept private.

With the advent of managed care in the early 1980s, everything changed. Psychiatrists, psychologists, and other providers of psychological services were now under contract with insurers (and/or their representatives and intermediaries, such as managed behavioral health companies), and were compelled by the terms of those contracts to participate in "utilization review." Practically speaking, this typically meant periodically making detailed disclosures of formerly confidential information about the clients to one or more case managers. Based on that information, which usually included diagnosis, history, presenting problems, progress, and treatment plan, case managers were empowered to authorize (or deny) ongoing psychological work. Disagreements between the service providers and case managers were common, and their resolutions often favored the cost-savings perspective of the case managers over those of the mental health professionals.

Since many case managers, at least at that time, had minimal training in psychology and psychotherapy, we therapists frequently complained (at least to one another) that nonprofessionals were making treatment decisions, sometimes cutting off reimbursement midtreatment and without warning. Clients were sometimes horrified to learn that the forms they signed to obtain insurance reimbursement included waivers of their confidentiality rights, and that insurers and employees of the insurance companies had access to their confidential treatment information.

Fast-forward to today. Third-party reimbursement methodologies have become increasingly complex, and the system is run by many different business models and multiple layers of bureaucracy that were unheard-of in the 1980s. But the basic concept remains the same: Psychologists and other mental health professionals are contracted providers, and as providers, we agree to provide only "medically necessary treatment" as authorized by the insurer. In some cases we are still required to formulate a diagnosis and treatment plan in order to make our case for "medical necessity," and confidential treatment information is utilized by an array of people in order to make decisions about the course of our clients' treatment. To make matters worse, contracted rates have generally been frozen for the past 20 years, so after taking inflation into account, providers' real income has decreased by as much as 50%.

Some insurance companies have given up on doing "utilization review," undoubtedly because they have found that the cost of providing such oversight is really not cost-effective. Others periodically try new approaches or recycle old approaches, alternating between telephonic, fax, e-mail, or Web-based treatment reviews. Recently colleagues have reported to me that they have received letters from insurers pointing out that they have been seeing a certain patient for X number of sessions, and they might want to consult with the insurance companies' professional staff. Honestly, I cannot imagine any of my peers voluntarily phoning any of the managed behavioral health companies to gain insights into how to provide more effective treatment! But as long as third parties are involved, the ultimate fate of that confidential information is beyond the control of the professional. Who does and who does not gain access to patient information depends on the policies and procedures of the administrative entity making the decisions about reimbursement, within the limits of current law.

"Diagnosis and treatment" constitutes the core language of the medical model. From the perspective of third-party payers, of course it makes sense to apply this same model to psychological treatment.

Health insurance is, after all, intended to pay medical bills when a person becomes sick or injured. So as long as our work is being reimbursed as part of one's medical insurance, psychotherapy will continue to be seen as a treatment for a medical condition. But this isn't the only way to think about our clients and their presenting problems; in fact, it may not even be the most productive way.

In the mid-1990s, I finally resigned from the preferred provider networks I had joined some years before. I realized that in the majority of instances I couldn't, in good conscience, make a case that my clients were psychologically ill: I too often found myself in the awkward position of agreeing with the insurer that my clients' requests for reimbursement should probably be denied.

Critiques of the *DSM* are widespread, widely known, and well reasoned on both scientific and philosophical grounds. I am typically in agreement with the perspective that says many of the *DSM* diagnostic categories represent artificial and poorly justified distinctions constructed between normal dimensions of human functioning. I'm not suggesting that all diagnosis is unjustified: Certainly some individuals suffer from significant disturbances such as major depression, schizophrenia, bipolar disorder, or other conditions that can be rightfully considered psychiatric disorders. However, I have found that I must ask myself again and again: How relevant is the concept of a disorder for most of my private clients? Do I feel confident about applying a *DSM*-based diagnosis when I recognize that this diagnosis will stay with him or her for life? Do I really believe this client is "mentally ill"?

Personally, I've concluded that not everything that looks like pathology is pathological, nor is every emotional pain, even persistent pain, necessarily a sign that something is broken and needs fixing. For example, while people stuck in an unhappy marriage may be in considerable distress, defenseless against certain unwelcome feelings, and completely paralyzed about what to do, I ask myself: Does this make them somehow psychologically unwell? Or are they just stuck? Ordinary human feelings like frustration, disappointment, sadness, and lack of enthusiasm can be mislabeled as depression. Likewise, worry, agitation, and fearfulness can sometimes be mislabeled as an anxiety disorder, just as run-of-the-mill shyness can be called a social phobia. We need to recognize that there are vast individual differences among healthy humans and that different doesn't mean disordered. Moreover, most of us believe that some emotional pain is normal, not pathological, and in fact needs to be accepted as part of life. This is certainly a core aspect of the mindfulness-based approaches, which have recently become popular, but this belief runs counter to our efforts to "diagnose and treat." And although many practitioners would say that they don't really take the *DSM* seriously, and they give a diagnosis in order to essentially "play the insurance game" that is required to be reimbursed, I think it is hard not to be at least subtly influenced by the pressures of playing the game, which reinforces the idea of psychopathology.

I have no quarrel with professionals whose psychological world-view is consistent with the *DSM*, and who are able to utilize the *DSM*-based diagnostic categories without internal conflict. However, I personally believe that most of the clients I have seen in my private practice are basically healthy and suffering from transient psychological confusion and/or pain. Diagnosis isn't really relevant for them, nor is the *DSM*.

The *DSM*'s 309-series codes, "adjustment disorders," are a set of broadly defined categories of normal functioning that include problems in living with various emotional sequelae. These codes do in fact seem relevant, although not particularly useful, for the vast majority of clients I've worked with in the past 25 years. Unlike other diagnostic codes, however, the 309-series codes don't really describe pathology, although they are characterized by "marked distress that is in excess of what would be expected from exposure to the stressor." But how do we decide what qualifies as excessive versus normal? Our primary approach of thinking about normality is (I hope!) primarily psychological, not statistical. Statistically, *excessive* refers to instances in the tails of some distribution curve. But psychologically, the amount of distress being experienced by any given person will almost certainly turn out to be exactly what would be expected for that person, at that time, under those circumstances. In a way, psychologically speaking, the idea of *excessive* distress is a bit absurd.

But if we're not treating mental disease, what are we doing? Here's my personal answer, which evolves out of my professional history: I have a PhD from Stanford University in developmental psychology. Before getting postdoctoral clinical training, obtaining a license, and starting my private practice, I spent more than a decade at Stanford doing research on normal adults and their children. The focus of my research was on the evolution of two-person relationships and on identifying ways that researchers might meaningfully differentiate relationships from one another. I also specialized in research methodology, statistics, and the philosophy of science. During my years at Stanford, I therefore learned a lot about normal human development and about normal, even exceptional, highly functioning two-person relationships. Just as importantly, I learned a lot about hypothesis generation, hypothesis testing, and the nature of scientific evidence. I learned to question everything, and to require overwhelming evidence before accepting that the conclusions drawn from some study are anything but figments of the researchers' imaginations. I learned that a high degree of well-reasoned skepticism is part of the scientific process.

All this has allowed my professional identity to evolve, so that I now represent myself as a psychologist, but not as a psychotherapist. I think of myself as a consultant, a teacher, a mentor, or a coach who works with normal, healthy people who want to improve their lives. Instead of thinking of my clients as mentally ill and of myself as a healer, I think of my clients as psychologically healthy individuals and couples seeking an unbiased, caring professional with a fresh pair of eyes and a fresh look at their situation.

My postdoctoral training in psychodynamic psychotherapy taught me how to think about the unfolding of the interpersonal process and about phenomena like transference and countertransference, projection, and identification as perfectly normal processes, affecting perfectly normal people. My postdoctoral training in cognitive-behavioral therapy taught me to think about how perfectly normal people sometimes conceptualize themselves and their problems in irrational, unhelpful ways, and how acting without thinking frequently accompanies irrational thinking. I continue to study approaches to psychotherapy and how people change, and apply what I learn in my work with normal, healthy individuals who are in a transient state of needing some help. Since the word *therapy* implies healing, and I don't conceptualize my clients as needing to be healed, I don't consider or market what I do as psychotherapy.

Of course, this means that my practice is a 100% fee-for-service practice. Since I don't do psychotherapy, I accept no reimbursement from insurance companies, and instead bill all fees directly to clients. I generally accept only clients whom I deem to be fundamentally psychologically healthy. What I actually do, however, isn't terribly different from what many psychotherapists do. I'm aware that my therapeutic style continues to have a psychodynamic feel to it, although it has evolved to be much more active and engaged than it used to be. I'm far more likely than I used to be to offer possible interpretations, suggestions, and homework assignments. I teach in the sense that I adopt a didactic stance in order to help clients understand what's happening in their lives. I'm less interested than I once was in insight for the sake of insight or the ideal cure, and am more aimed at helping my clients obtain tangible, measurable results.

Although I maintain written records similar to those that would be required of licensed psychotherapists, these records, since they do not describe treatment, are not medical records and are consequently of no interest to any insurance companies, insurance adjusters, or anyone else. They are genuinely confidential records. And although my practice is Health Insurance Portability and Accountability Act (HIPAA) compliant, strictly speaking HIPAA doesn't apply to me, either, because mine are not health records. I continue to practice exclusively within the limits of my training, experience, and competence. I am very clear to prospective clients about what we can do together, and about what we will not be doing. By rendering the split between the healer and the healed irrelevant, I meet my clients as a collaborator. My client relationships feel stronger than ever, and more interpersonally authentic.

I offer this perspective simply as a way of sharing my journey as a helping professional, not as a prescription of how other therapists should think about or practice their craft. And to reiterate an important point: I do not by any means deny the existence of mental illness.

Rather, I notice that it's extremely rare in clients who seek help in a private, fee-for-service practice. I also am aware that by refusing to accept insurance, I am making myself much less available to individuals who would find it economically difficult or even prohibitive to pay for my services. But for me this is the only way of operating a practice that feels congruent with my conceptualization of who my clients are and how they change—and I feel grateful that my *DSM-*free practice has continued to thrive. More generally, I believe that our training as psychologists makes us well suited to offer a wide range of valuable services to the public, and that psychotherapy is only one of them. We are here to help our clients, and there are many different ways to do that.

ABOUT JOHN A. MARTIN, PHD

John Martin is a licensed psychologist in San Francisco. He has been practicing for more than 25 years. He received his PhD from Stanford University and spent many years as a teacher and researcher there before turning to full-time independent private-practice work. For more information about John or to contact him, please visit his website at http://jamartin.com.

This article was originally published by Psychotherapy.net and we are grateful for their permission to share this with you.

About David Steele

AUTHOR, RELATIONSHIP COACHING PIONEER,
AND GLOBAL AUTHORITY ON GROWING A
PROFITABLE PRIVATE PRACTICE

After two decades serving as a couples therapist in full-time private
practice, David Steele grew weary of trying to save marriages and
chase insurance reimbursements to survive. He discovered personal
life coaching in 1996. Within three months of completing his initial
coach training, he had transformed his therapy practice into a thriving and profitable coaching practice. He subsequently created and
tested a standardized model for relationship coaching that is the
foundation for the curriculum taught at the Relationship Coaching
Institute (RCI), the first and largest relationship coach training
organization in the world. Steele and his team at RCI have since

trained thousands of relationship coaches and mentored hundreds of therapists and coaches to build successful, sustainable practices that guide their clients to enjoy more satisfying, functional lives so they can make a difference in the world. His practical advice about how to grow and sustain a profitable, rewarding coaching practice gives struggling therapists cause for hope and celebration.

A prolific writer and creator of proprietary and proven coaching models, mentoring programs, and practice-building products such as *Private Practice Magic* and *Private Practice Marketing on a Budget*, Steele is an industry pioneer and a sought-after speaker and trainer who is passionate about showing therapists a better way to achieve lasting success and significance. As he often says, "It doesn't matter where you've been. What matters is where you're going and how you'll get there."

Steele is happily married to his soul mate Darlene and parent to three children, including twin boys. He lives in Northern California.